Tulips and Tales
from
The Golden Age

A childhood in communist Romania, 1975-1989

Camelia Andrei

For Sofia and Elisabetta

CONTENTS

ACKNOLEDGEMENTS

A massive thank you goes to my university professor Guido Candela, and his beloved wife professor Grazia Mezzetti, who helped me with the copywriting and encouraged me to publish this book in Italy in 2013.

I would like to express my gratitude to my friend Chris Tyas, engineer by brain and poet by soul, who gave me the inspiration and encouraged me to translate this book into English during Covid-19 crisis.

A big thank you to my copywriter Jonathan Campion, who helped me to bring this book to life in English language.

I must say thank you to Mrs. Jeanette Murell, my daughter's English teacher, who kindly offered to have a last proof read of the manuscript before publishing it.

FOREWORD

Everyone lived through Romania's last years of communism between 1980s and 1989, in their own way. In this book I share my memories, and tell my stories, with the innocence of the child I was at the time. Those of us who remember this period can now, more or less, look back and smile, recalling the atmosphere, the sensations and the objects that surrounded us. We remember the people, their habits, and sometimes bizarre ways of doing things.

For most Romanians of my generation, these stories may evoke distant memories. For those who didn't experience 'Romania's golden age', I hope to let the feel a little of what is was like.

I have collected all my stories in this book, to be read by you and my daughters, and, most importantly, so that they will not be forgotten. With all its advantages and disadvantages, this period is part of my life. It taught me how to appreciate the little things, as well as the big things in life. It taught me how to face difficult situations, and helped me to become who I am today. It is the umbilical cord that still connects me with my homeland, even now that I am so far away.

It is not my intention to offend anyone's memory with these stories. These are just the events as I experienced them. Some people's names have been changed to protect their identities and privacy.

CHAPTER 1

LIFE IN BUZAU

BLOCK OF FLATS No. 2

I was born in 1972. I grew up with my mother and father in a good neighbourhood in the town of Buzău, a collection of four and ten-floor buildings, a two-hour drive east of Bucharest, in the Baragan plain. I was two when my parents moved from their studio flat on the outskirts of the town to a new one-bedroom apartment in 'Block of Flats no.2'.

My mother, Rodica, was always a good looking woman. She was very young when she had me. She was an only child, like me, and she came from a family with very rigid and authoritarian principles. Her father, my grandfather, had noble origins: in March 1961, when the communists took over the country with Gheorghe Gheorghiu Dej, he was expropriated of all his estates and goods, which he owned in the centre of Bucharest. At the same time he was dismissed from the Military Forces, accused of being the son of a legionnaire of the Green Shirts[1]. The communists even forced him to change his surname: Jager was considered too "foreign", so he became Iagaru, which sounded more Romanian. My grandfather lived for the rest of his life with great psychological trauma, which took a toll on his family as well as his health.

He was hit by an unknown illness later in life, which forced my grandmother to literally carry him on her tiny shoulders

---

[1] The Green Shirts were part of the Iron Guard, the nationalist movement, against capitalism, against bolshevism and against Judaism, founded by Corneliu Zelea Codreanu in 1930.

from room to room, and from the third floor of their flat to the bench in front of their building, for at least 14 years. That illness today is known as Parkinson's disease.

I regret that I couldn't do anything to allow him to live better, such as buying him a wheelchair. These were not available in the shops at the time, and the hospitals wouldn't provide one. For as long as he had the strength, my grandfather continued to read books, despite his shaking hands. Almost every time I went to see him, he asked me to go to Bucharest – George Cosbuc Street, number 5 – to see the house where he was born, in 1929. It was where he grew up with his father, his mother and a couple of servants.

After high school, my mother never looked for a job; she preferred to be a housewife. With a desire to leave home, and to get away from my grandfather's mood swings, she married my father as soon as she finished school. Not long after their wedding, I was born, on the day in October when the Army was celebrated with a national holiday. This made my father even more proud.

As a military pilot, by law my father couldn't own private properties. Our 40 square-metre apartment was government property, and was given to him by the Army. There was only a small monthly charge to pay, based on the flat's size and the number of people living in it. On top of this we were charged for utilities consumption, which was limited to a certain amount, above which we were charged more than double. Keeping an eye on all the meters, especially the electric one, was like a daily sport. In the following years the situation with electricity became even worse, as the limit was set lower and lower. But I will tell you this story in another chapter.

We lived here, between Union Boulevard and Karl Marx Street, in apartment 7, for about ten years, from 1974 until 1984. And it was here that we faced an earthquake on 4th of March 1977 that measured 7.3 on the Richter scale. The earthquake destroyed half of the city of Bucharest, and caused over 1,500 deaths across the whole country. After this tragic event, dozens of beautiful listed buildings were declared unsafe and deliberately demolished – not because they couldn't be made safe again, but because they had been getting in the way of bigger communist projects. After the earthquake, there were rumors about missing people in mysterious conditions. They were not any people, they were important people, actors, writers, journalists, considered uncomfortable for the Regime. Some beautiful churches have been demolished too, blamed of staying in the way of the progress, same as those people.. Although I was only five at the time, I remember the fear in people's eyes, as they ran out, some of them naked, from the ten-storey building in front of ours. That building was moving like a corn plant in a windy field. Long cracks opened up inside its external and internal walls, big enough to put your hand through. At one point I could see into our neighbours' living room.

But these buildings were left standing, and nobody bothered to check their safety. At least I have no memory of anyone doing so, and we and all our neighbours continued to live there for several more years. Just like us, our building resisted too, standing for many years to come. It is still there, surrounded by the same poplars that my father planted more than 40 years ago.

MY FATHER

My father, Dumitru known as Andy, was a military pilot. This had been his dream since he was a small boy, and he worked hard to make it happen. While he studied at high school he also worked as a painter and decorator – the reason I have always had a good opinion of men who can do DIY. He was a stubborn man, with a tough and tenacious character. After military school he attended the Bucharest Military Academy. From there began his career, starting as a captain, then becoming a major. He rose to become a colonel, only one step away from the highest military grade of general. He earned good money at the time. Every 23rd day of the month he came home with his salary in a bag, which he used to display on our living room table in piles of tens, twenty–fives, fifties and hundreds. All three of us shared out the money, based on our monthly expenses. The last task was to distribute our savings using little books provided by the House of Savings, *Casa de Economii si Consemnatiuni* (CEC for short).

The CEC was an important institution – a sort of public piggy bank, connected with the National Bank, to which only state institutions had access. The CEC allowed you to have good interest rates, based on the terms of your deposits, which could have been for three or six months or one year. Definitely they were more complex but this is what I remember about them.

I used to have an account of my own, which is why this monthly meeting was very important for me too. My father used to give me a hundred *lei* note to deposit into my book. Seeing my pot filling with hundred notes month by month made me very proud.

I remember those years as a very happy part of my childhood, thanks to my parents, who managed to give me everything I needed to grow up in a healthy and happy environment. But not everybody was as lucky as I was, so I feel it's necessary to introduce you to the bigger picture of those years. I can tell you about the food items we couldn't find in the shops, and how you could get your hands on them, but not through the simple process that you are probably used to today. Having an additional piece of bread on top of our family's daily ratio, or a slice of salami on the table, wasn't easy, and took a ton of patience and good luck. Food scarcity was our life companion. It was the main factor that influenced our habits from the second half of the 1970s onwards.

THE FOOD SHOP

Sometimes in the food shop – which was called the *alimentara* – you were able to find the 'free' products, as they used to be called. These were the items that weren't rationed; for which you didn't have to use your monthly ticket. Until 1984 we had only a bread ticket for our daily use, while other items were sold directly to the public from the shops' shelves. Apart from the beans, peas, beans and sausages in cans, which were so loved by the workers on building sites, there was also fruit in tin cans of syrup, and tins with 'Eat Oceanic Fish' on them – which nowadays would be something like a marketing slogan. So many of these words hadn't even been part of our vocabulary before. Advertising on the TV or radio was unknown to us. You could find Vietnamese prawn crackers, 'summer salami', and the famous *parizer* – a sort of pink, 15-centimetre wide creamy mashed meat, which was the consistency of a hot dog, and spiced and flavoured with unknown potions. They were a delight for Romanians, especially for us children. *Parizer* sandwiches became our school lunches.

Shops also sold smoked sausages. They used to look great but my mother, not trusting what was inside them, never bought them. Rarely shops were supplied with red and yellow Kogeak sweets, similar to the better-known Chupa-Chups, but much bigger, and covered with a simple transparent cellophane. For these there was a limit of one kilo per person, but that was a lot, and in the end mum used to buy me about 10 of them, making my playmates green with envy.

At the supermarket checkout you could find, for the price of one *lei*, chewing gum in two formats: razor-blade shape or cigarette shape. Both of them crumbled straight away in your mouth and were always a waste of time, not to mention the pain going up to your ears as you tried to make them chewy and elastic. The alimentara shop was part of a bigger structure, called a 'complex'. I imagine this name came from its very complicated layout, because they brought together in one place many other shops – the greengrocers, the bakery, the barber shop, the tobacconist, the shop for stationary and beauty products, etc. There was no imagination to any of this: the shops were simply named after the items inside. So a shop that sold shoes was called 'Shoe Shop'; the greengrocer was 'Fruit and Veg Shop', and so on. The only exception was the general shop, the big shop, which was located in the very centre of every town in Romania, next to the city council and the city hotel. Our general shop in Buzău was called Dacia, the ancient name for our land, and the only car brand that was produced in Romania (in cooperation with Renault) at the time. Actually, Dacia was the land inhabited by the Dacians since the fourth century BC. The Greeks referred to them as the Getae (east of Dacia) and the Romans called them Daci. Compared with the general shop 'Bucur Obor' in Bucharest, Dacia offered a much smaller choice of items. Some of its departments were completely empty.

Next to it was the Council Palace and Hotel Pietroasa, an eight-floor building usually frequented by foreigners and politicians. On the ground floor was a shop that was just called 'Shop', in English. This place was off-limits for Romanians. It was only for tourists from abroad, and the only money accepted was American dollars. It had the most beautiful shop window in town, behind which were products that were out of our reach: Tic–Tacs; cans of Dab beer and

Coke; Spearmint and Brooklyn chewing gum; Toblerone chocolate; Nutella; American peanuts and coffee; Kent, Marlboro and Pall Mall cigarettes; perfumes and soaps; and many other items from seemingly another world. The packaging and the lighting made the shop sparkle and shine, and on dark nights during the monitored electricity blackouts it was like a festive lighting display. We weren't allowed inside 'Shop', so we could only spy a little through the double security windows, when the bodyguard in front of it wasn't looking. Eventually I could take a better look at these otherworldly goods, thanks to my father. But that's for another chapter.

With the completion of a massive new development along Union Boulevard, many new ground-floor shops opened, facing the town's main street: a shop for carpets and rugs; a perfume shop; an auto parts shop (with a section entirely dedicated to Dacia parts); a coffee shop; a shop selling socks and tights, and a fishmonger, which was almost always empty.

One day, behind our complex, opened a tiny shop with very noisy and bulky machinery inside. Here you could fill a bottle with soda water, in change of 50 or 80 bani (there were 100 bani in a leu). Most of the bottles were made of stainless steel; the original ones were made of glass and protected by a metal mesh, but they were rare finds. We still had one original bottle; the other one was an 8-litre heavy stainless steel cylinder, with a diameter of about 20cm, which was painful to carry every time my parents sent me to refill it. The shop was only five minutes from our flat, but the walk took me 20 minutes. This was one of the children's jobs, as well as throwing out the smelly rubbish bags. I used to do one of these about every three days.

And the rubbish smelled awful, because we didn't use plastic bags to protect the bucket. Plastic bags were hard to find: they used to be jealously guarded, and used only on special occasions, such as for birthday presents or Christmas gifts.

Some afternoons I used to go to the food shop to buy *pufarine* and *fulgi de porumb:* cereals and cornflakes. I remember that we used to eat them dry, out of their packages, because nobody told us how they were supposed to be eaten. We had no promotion on telly. I only found out many years later that cereals are meant to be eaten with milk. Sometimes we could find 'Cip' sweets; in reality these were sprinkles to decorate cakes with, but no one told us what they were for either, so we just licked them out of their plastic box. We had our own soft drinks, too: 'Quik' was a poor copy of Pepsi Cola; 'Brifcor' was a sort of orange fizzy drink. Whenever we went to Bucharest, my father used to buy me the 'Cico' orange fizzy drink, or the real Pepsi Cola, which you could only find in the big cities and in restaurants. Another very popular sweet was gingerbread, which was made in 6-centimetre square shapes. It was so hard that you could break your teeth on it if you didn't suck on it for a few minutes before biting into it.

CHILDREN AND CHEESE

I was about seven or eight years old. It was a morning of my summer holiday, and as usual I was playing with my friends in front of our building. It was stiflingly hot outside, over 38 degrees centigrade, without any sort of cooling breeze. The trees were like the decorative elements of an impressionist painting. Life was rolling in slow motion: the few people outside were walking quietly and lazily. This almost enchanted atmosphere was broken by shouts from Marius, a kid from the second floor, announcing an event that would break the day out of its slumber: 'The cheese is coming! The cheese is coming! At the complex, the cheese is *coooming*!' Without thinking twice I ran to my mother. I asked her to give me 10 lei and, almost breathless, I ran to the alimentara shop, where people from every part of the neighbourhood had already started to congregate behind the store, where the deliveries arrived. Cheese was a precious item, and more difficult to find than many other food products. It was almost unnecessary to unload it from the truck and put it on the shop's shelves. They used to sell it straight from the back of the truck –it was quicker, easier and more efficient.

People nowadays often mention 'queues', but in reality it was just a crowd of people. This afternoon I was the seventh closest – an achievement I was very proud of. But I was on the wrong side of a rusty metal mesh fence, while some shop assistants came out to see how many people were waiting. Someone asked if it was really true that the cheese was arriving, but they didn't bother to answer our questions, simply shrugging their shoulders.

They knew that the cheese was on its way, but were told to not tell us, so that even more people wouldn't show up. The shop assistants were also involved in a sort of a black market. They used to sell food 'under hand', as we called it, or 'under the till', to friends, family members and important people. Having a food shop assistant as a friend was precious: you wouldn't want to lose their friendship for anything.

After a few hours of waiting, on this boiling hot summer afternoon, I remember how I began to feel the weight of the crowd on my tiny shoulders, because more and more people were now arriving, pushing to gain a better position in the scrum. Next to me a second and a third line was quickly appearing. I was already very familiar with the six people in front of me, but now more impatient people were there to steal my place. My precious seventh place! The pressure was growing, and my left arm was being pressed into the metal mesh fence. I had to push back with my whole body to avoid being squashed by the crowd, which by this point had become agitated from the long wait and the temperature.

After almost six hours of waiting, finally the supply truck with the white cheese – a sort of feta, immersed in a sour liquid – arrived. But this was the worst moment: Marius's rumour had been true after all, and now people from all over the neighbourhood were in a frenzy. I wasn't the seventh in line anymore, maybe the twentieth, thanks to the complete chaos created by new people surging into the queue. They were arguing, swearing, pushing; everybody was insulting everybody else. Somebody fainted, but was still standing up, ignoring the law of gravity. At this point I couldn't feel my arm anymore. It had turned a shade of blue, as the blood wasn't circulating properly. My cheek was in the same condition, but at least I was still breathing while keeping tight the 10 lei note.

Once the provisory sales counter was sorted, a little table positioned against the fence (which had a 20-centimetre hole cut into it to pass food through on these extraordinary occasions), the lady at the till shouted at the crowd: 'Only half kilo per person!' Good, I said to myself. A few more minutes and I could go back home with a nice chunk of fresh, white, sour and smelly *telemea* cheese. Gosh, it was so good on fresh bread, with a slice of tomato and cucumber; or just grated on top of chips, as my father loved to make them. I was salivating at the thought of it. Half an hour later, my turn finally came. The woman at the till was in her thirties, and had a very serious face. She watched all of us with an air of superiority, like a cockerel in a chicken coop.

I asked her for my half kilo of cheese. Her voice came back at me like an unexplainable thunder in a sunny day: 'We do not sell to children!'

For an instant I felt faint. All the nasty moments during those hours in the crowd came back into my head: the heat, the sun, my painful arm, the pushing, the shouting, the swearing, the infinite patience, the resilience, the resistance.. What was the meaning of all that? I felt like I had to do something. I had to react somehow. But the only thing I was able to say, in between my tears and hiccups, was: 'It's not fair! It's not fair!' Nobody defended me. The queue continued its course, unaware of my suffering or my feelings. Everyone was only worried about their spot in the queue and their own piece of cheese.

BREAD, MILK AND MEAT

As I have mentioned, the complex was home to the bakery, the milk and cheese shop and the butchers. But people mostly came every day for the bread. The bakery was the only shop where people used to respect a queue, which moved quickly even if you had 40 people in front of you. You would show the shop assistant your monthly ticket – a card coloured a different colour for each month, with a day-by-day chart drawn on it – and once you had received your daily ration of bread, the assistant would tick that day off.

The ration was half a loaf of bread, which weighed about 400 grams, per family member per day. Sometimes it wasn't baked enough and the middle of it was just a ball of dough. But no-one ever complained: it just meant it was a bad day. Mine was a family of three, so our daily ration was a loaf and a half. My mother always told me to ask for a well-baked piece of bread. But the real problems with bread came when you had to celebrate a birthday or a baptism, or any other event. All you could do then was to ask your friends or neighbours to give you their leftover bread. And that was a nightmare, believe me..

The bread supply was limited, and it wasn't always enough. Sometimes there was no bread on the shelves at all. My mother, as a housewife, was always informed in time about new deliveries, and on those unlucky occasions when we were late and there was no bread left – as the shop assistant was her friend – she could always get a piece of bread under the counter. This friend helped us a lot in those dark days.

Next to the bread counter was the milk and cheese one, which by 9am was already empty of any sort of food, until the following morning at 7am, when a very small amount of milk, sour cream, cottage cheese and yoghurt was delivered. People started queuing from 6am, or even earlier. I remember those little glass jars with a foil lid on top. Sometimes they delivered butter and margarine, in little packs of 45 grams each. The butter was full of water: you had to drain it out before you used it. It was also very hard to spread on bread, so my mother used to toast a slice of bread in a pan first, to defeat this strange dairy product.

The good thing about the dairy products was that we didn't need a ticket to buy them. But the shop itself had rules about the maximum amount of each item that could be purchased. We were allowed no more than two litres of milk per purchase (sometimes only one), no more than one jar of sour cream or cottage cheese, a couple of jars of yoghurt, and one pack of butter. If the pack was a 100 grams one, the shop assistant would cut it in half. The milk was handed over only in glass bottles; to be given one you had to give an empty one in exchange. Empty milk bottles were worth their weight in gold.

The other important shop in our complex was the butcher's. It was the most deserted shop you could ever imagine. The shelves were always empty, morning and evening, but it had its moments. Despite the bare shelves, people were always queuing in front of it. Most of them were pensioners, and they used to bring with them small chairs and even blankets from home when the weather was cold. Pensioners had a lot of free time, and for them it was better in front of the shop than at home. Here they used to socialise, make new friends, and chat and gossip about the neighbourhood. Day or night, they used to save spots for one another if somebody needed to leave for a few hours.

You may be asking why they chose the butcher's to gather in front of. Well, the butcher shop didn't have its own 'grapevine', to warn people when new deliveries came in. Getting your hands on some meat was a complete lottery, with only a few lucky days every month. And this meat could arrive in any form: nothing but bones; chicken; nothing but fat; mashed scraps; sometimes some real beef or pork. And these elderly people, with not much to do in their lonely homes, stayed there with great tenacity, hoping that, just maybe, Thursday could be their day. This queue was off-limits for me as a child.

In our Romanian universe, the connotation of the word 'meat' was different. For us 'meat' was anything that had once been part of a pig, cow or chicken. It didn't necessarily have any meat on it. The butcher's was supplied with turkey bones, *'tacamùri'*: people hilariously pronounced the word with a Japanese accent, to emphasise its foreign (or should I say unknown) origins. They were literally just bones, without a trace of meat left on them. But our mothers, miracle-workers that they were, were able to cook the best soup ever with them, by boiling the bones for hours to squeeze any last flavour of meat from them. Romanian cuisine is traditionally based on soups called *ciorbe* – a *'must'* if eaten at lunchtime. Just as Italians have hundreds of sorts of pasta, so we Romanians have hundreds of soups. Each region has its own secret recipes.

Sometimes the delivery was all about pork parts: pork fat, pigs' heads, and half-smoked pig's trotter called 'Adidas' by some for obvious reasons. Sometimes it was chicken, which for whatever reason wasn't good enough to export. Romania farmed chickens mainly for the Chinese market, one of our most important trade partners. The problem was that these products never arrived together, so you had to be happy with one of them at a time. The limit was usually two kilos per person, and the supply was limited to satisfy only 40 to 60 people. At least this queue was the most polite.

At the end of the seventies the gaps between deliveries became longer and longer. The old people used to spend weeks in the queue, with a hope that they never lost, to buy just one kilo of something meaty.

My parents and I were a bit luckier than others, because my

father, as a military pilot, by law had to consume a certain amount of proteins, carbohydrates and sugars per month. Until 1984 he had to consume 4,500 calories per day, then 5,500, based on the sort of airplanes and helicopters he used to fly.

All the food he couldn't eat inside the military base canteen during the holidays, weekends and other days off, it was accumulated and it was given to take home. Amounts were all strictly calculated in the top secret military offices.

I remember that massive bag full of goodies, like dark chocolate, tins of fish, vegetables, butter, salami, cheese, jams, coffee; things that were almost impossible to find in shops. Counting the chocolate bars was my favourite hobby. I had a sort of chocolate bar collection, which I jealously hid inside a doll box. Dark chocolate wasn't my favourite flavour, but there wasn't much choice, and the milk chocolate, tiny golden bars from China, were very rare.

Fresh food, such as salami and cheese, were the first to be eaten. My father was allowed 40 grams of salami per day, and 400 grams of real meat. Our cupboard was always full of food, as well as our fridge and freezer. Thankfully, queuing for food wasn't a big concern for my mother or for me.

WINTER CANNING

During the winter the shelves of the fruit and veg shop (the *aprozar*) were empty for months. September was the perfect time to start thinking about winter supplies. The farmers market and the *aprozar* were where you could buy tens of kilos of aubergines, peppers, onion, potatoes, cucumber, tomatoes, carrots, cabbages, apples and quinces. The farmers market, was the public market for fruit and veg usually located in a central position within the city centre. The farmers could sell there all the products that they were producing, herbs, garlic, carrots, watermelons, corn, dried beans, milk, cheese and cream sometimes. All these items were what we would now call organic. And it needed to be tens of kilos, because there was a lot of cooking involved to fill up the cupboards for the cold weather. I don't think importing fruit and veg during the winter was on our government's to-do list.

Autumn was the time to dust off the old notebooks, full of recipes handed down in the family, and prepare preserves, tasty jams and fruit mustards. You could buy as many vegetables as you could carry, so having a car with a big boot or a big family with strong arms was an advantage.

The amount of fruit and veg in our houses at that time of the year was an industrial one, worthy of a small canning factory. In my home there were 40 kilos of potatoes, stored under sand in a corner of our balcony to stop them from freezing; 20 or 30 kilos of cabbage, stored in a grey plastic barrel and covered with salty water, herbs and spices. There were also lots of green tomatoes, carrots and cauliflowers, preserved in a special brine. There was an art to canning, and my mother was a true artist. The 10- and 20-litre glass jars became a canvas for her artwork: carrots cropped in the shape of flowers and stars; cauliflowers and peppers all placed carefully in a geometric pattern. That was the measure of her talent and culinary skills. Some of our neighbours also used to display their jars on their balconies, so that the whole neighbourhood could appreciate their creations.

Empty beer bottles had a second use during the winter. They became perfect containers for homemade tomato sauce, or for vegetable sauces used to enrich the soups. The different size jars were also used for jams made from prunes, quinces, green nuts, or for a tasty *zacusca*. *Zacusca* is a sort of stew made mainly from aubergines, peppers and onions. It was boiled slowly for hours before being poured in the jars, and sterilised in the oven on top of stainless kitchen knives, in order to avoid any unpleasant waste. Every family had its own secret ingredients, and sometimes the mums changed their recipe to impress friends and family. The trend in my home was to use forest mushrooms, the little ones, instead of aubergine. The result was exquisite.

At the beginning of October our larder was full, with perfectly aligned jars, sorted by size and colour, each one with a hand-written label and curly cellophane lids.

Separate freezers didn't exist at the time. We only had a single frozen shelf in our fridges, so preserving and canning food for winter helped us a lot.

LIFE IN THE NEIGHBOURHOOD

Behind our building there was a nice garden, which was enclosed on purpose to stop children like us from damaging the grass and flowers. In front of it was Karl Marx street, where in one corner was *Tataia*'s house. Tataia means grandfather in Romanian, and this is what we called this very old and skinny man, with hair the colour of snow. Tataia was in his proud eighties, a veteran of the First and Second World War. You could read the stories of his past in his wise eyes. We used to knock on his green wooden gates. A few minutes later he would open the gate with a basket full of fruits and chestnuts from his garden. He knew why we were there, and he never disappointed us. We would give him a quick thank you and then run back to our games, like little naughty thieves.

When Tataia died, all the children from our neighbourhood went to his house, to see his body in a coffin on the table of his living room, as per our awkward Orthodox tradition. For us it was more out of curiosity than to pay respects to such a lovely old man; we used to go to see the bodies of all our neighbours who passed away. Their houses were opened to the public for three days for a sort of procession, so that anybody could pay tribute to the deceased person. This is not something I would happily do nowadays, not least because I have since developed a sort of phobia of dead bodies, and I am afraid of the dark and of being alone in the house. There is always an explanation for our fears, and I think that these ones are quite connected to that period of my childhood.

Despite this, I still keep the memory of dear Tataia, and his sunny allotment, in my heart.

The corner of Karl Marx street was also a meeting place for us in the summer. It was along the route to the seaside – on the way towards the Black Sea for those coming from the north or west of the country. To our joy, it wasn't just Romanians travelling this way, but Polish tourists too. Their Baltic Sea wasn't as warm as our coastline during the summer, and they preferred to spend their summer holidays here. It was also cheaper for them, and as foreigners in our country they were treated well. The Poles were still living in a communist country too, of course, but they had many more privileges than us. One of these privileges was the chance to travel abroad. They used to cross into Czechoslovakia, then Hungary, and then travel through the whole of Romania to reach the Danube Delta, and the uninterrupted 244 kilometres of Black Sea beach. Their most popular car was the Fiat 126, and these were painted in happy shades of orange, green and red. Some of them even drove in massive caravans. We used to wait, for hours sometimes, under the hot sun, to see the Polish cars turning into our street on their way to the sea. Marius, the kid from the second floor, was usually the first to spot them from far away: 'The foreigners are coming! The foreigners are coming!' He was our first wireless communication device. This migration was an important event during those hot days, because the Polish tourists, knowing that we were less fortunate than their own children, used to throw sweets from their car windows. They weren't allowed to stop their cars: 'somebody' forbade it, and if they were caught talking to us, they could have been sent back to Poland immediately, with a stamp in their passports saying that they had been expelled from Romania.

Our favourite outdoor games were hide and seek and *Cartoane* – throwing a flat stone at a little cardboard tower, which was made from little cards retrieved from matchboxes. The stone was the key, so once you found a good one, you had to hide it somewhere at home, where your mother couldn't find it. The more times you knocked down the cardboard towers, the better your reputation as a *Cartoane* player became. You could exchange them as well, like children nowadays do with trading cards. Sometimes instead of *Cartoane* we used to play *tablitze*, which was almost the same game, but with stacks of flattened caps of beer bottles. But this was more of a boys' game.

Then there were games that children played in groups, like 'Parola', 'Country, Country, We Need Soldiers', 'Statues', 'Fat Milk', 'The Goat', 'The Stone Bridge', 'La Metrò Qui Passe' (I think this was a French game, because we had to sing along in French), and a miming game when we became teenagers. We also liked to lie on little blankets in the garden in front of the building, and play with toys and dolls, inventing stories of happy families, hospitals and dead people.

We were allowed to play in the garden in front of our building because my father was the only person who took care of it. He built a fence, planted about six poplars on the edge, and a weeping willow in the middle. From old airplane tires he made lovely flower pots, and painted them in all sorts of colours. Our garden was a triumph of colours, daisies, lion's mouth flowers, daffodils, roses… a paradise for bees, and an enchanted corner of our neighbourhood, which became more beautiful every year. All our neighbours had a special admiration for my father. He was a much respected man, and a solemn man as well. My mother used to supervise us from the kitchen window, where she used to spend most of the day.

Our kitchen was very small, but there was enough space for a fridge, a table against the wall with three chairs, the sink and the hob. The kitchen was the heartbeat of the flat: it was there that my mother used to play host to her best friends over a cup of *Nechezol*, a drink made like Turkish coffee. *Nechezol* was a poor man's coffee, and was made with roasted barley grains instead of real coffee beans. Real coffee was a luxury: not everyone had access to it. My mother and her friends used to read the future with the 'coffee' grounds in the bottom of their cups, or spend time knitting or crocheting. Sometimes our kitchen became an art studio, where my mother used to paint. She used to paint flowers − a lot of flowers − landscapes, and horses in the middle of angry waves. My father was in charge with the frames and the canvas preparation. He was really pleased to help and he dedicated a lot of his time to build frames of all sizes. Our family friends loved her paintings, and she was usually overrun with orders. Our walls were covered with her paintings, like a small art gallery. She earned very good money from selling them, with her prices going from three hundred to a thousand lei. But she struggled with her mental health at the time, and couldn't always focus on her creativity, so sometimes there were gaps of months between one painting and the next. Sometimes she was able to paint five in a row, and sometimes there was nothing for months. She used to say that it was because of a lack of inspiration, or not enough natural light coming through the window. The money she earned from selling her paintings went towards my growing collection of dolls, or her collection of shoes. My father never asked her what she did with that money, as long as she was happy.

THE DREADED NEIGHBOURS

Even our nice neighbourhood had its 'bad' neighbours. We were terrified of some of them. One of them was Mr Sawisky, a man with a big fat belly and a little limp. We nicknamed him Patlagica (green tomato), due to his big fat nose marked by little purple holes. Mr Sawisky lived on the ground floor of building number one, in the middle of which was a street lamp, the only source of light for a hundred metres. He was retired, and spent all his time in his pyjamas, sitting outside on his improvised green painted bench and playing backgammon with whoever would play with him.

After the 1977 earthquake, most of the houses facing Unirii Boulevard were suddenly demolished, despite the fact that they could be repaired. It was to make space for bigger, socialist housing blocks: a new row of eight- and nine-floor buildings. The neighbourhood's peace and quiet was interrupted for a few years, and the area in front of our building became a dirty building site, full of hazards and dangers, especially for us children. The equipment and industrial machinery, bulldozers, cranes, excavators made a lot of noise. Our beautiful garden was filled with dust, and my father had to water the plants almost every day to save them.

During the workers' lunch break we were supposed to have a bit of peace, but instead of the lovely sound of silence, we heard the sound of dice and shouting, as our neighbours played noisy board games. There were always at least four people playing, sometimes with others standing over them to watch. I think they organised championships, and they bet money and beers as well. They clearly had a lot of fun, and nobody dared to tell them off. After all, nobody could face old Sawisky. There was more: he hated children. We were his worst nightmare. If for any reason one of us needed to walk past his door (which was always half-open) we had to go on our tiptoes and hold our breath. If he spotted us he would throw shoes at us, or whatever else he had close by. Once he threw a bucket of cold water on us.

I used to run that gauntlet quite often, because on that floor lived my mother's best friend Rica. Her husband was a crane driver and was at work until six o'clock from Monday to Saturday. Rica and he had a love-hate relationship, with highs and lows. My mother and Rica used to go to see one another for a gossip and a cup of *Nechezol* when my father and her husband were at work. When my mother went to her flat, she would bring me too, and I had to pass terrified in front of that half-opened door.

Then there was Mrs. Codreanu, a tiny lady with an evergreen chignon on top of her head who lived on the second floor. Her husband was tall and skinny, very serious and a man of few words, but quite respected in our neighbourhood. I can't say the same about his wife: we all thought she was horrible. We hated her and her evil thin lips at least as much as Mr Sawisky. As soon as she heard our voices in the back yard, where her apartment faced, she would shout at us. Sometimes she even ran down the stairs with a stick in her hand to scare us. But we were quicker than her, and usually managed to hide from her. But sometimes she came unexpectedly. If she caught one of us, she pulled us by the ears so hard that they stayed red for a long time afterwards. We would cry from the pain. She caught me once, and my mother got so angry with her they never spoke again. But I realise now that we weren't very nice to her either. We would make her a target for our pea-shooters. Maybe we deserved her treatment…

THE PAIRED PHONE

One day technicians came to install our land line; definitely an important event. My mother, using her powers of seduction, persuaded the men to give us the red phone with a white disk, not the grey one that most people got. These red telephones were very rare: they would be collectors' items today.

To get your phone installed quicker, without being on the

waiting list for months, you had to make a compromise: have it paired with somebody else's. Our next-door neighbours agreed to set up a paired line with us, and we got a landline installed faster than anybody else. But there were downsides to this friendly arrangement. When our neighbour was using the phone, we had to wait until the line was free to make our own call. When we were talking with somebody they could spy on our conversation. If we had to make an urgent call while they were using the phone, we used to knock on the wall to ask them to free the line. Sometimes we got their phone calls and they got ours. I still remember our first telephone number: 39 700. It was really easy to remember, and was placed on the little window display in our living room, for all to see, because not everybody at that time could own such a luxury item, or afford such an extra monthly expense.

Phone calls were anonymous. You couldn't see what number was calling you, as you can today, so prank phone calls became a trend. People would call random numbers and not say anything, or say rude words, or make funny noises. But the worst ones were the blackmail calls – unknown voices telling you about your wife or husband's affairs. That was just spiteful. If this happened often you could ask the line supplier to put your phone under surveillance (at an extra cost, of course). It was the only way to get the person to stop annoying you.

CUSTOMS AND TRADITIONS

The Christmas celebrations were my favourite time of the year. We started the countdown from the beginning of December, not in September as happens now. The beginning of December was a good time to start planning and organising. It was when I could open my father's military suitcase, where we kept all the decorations.

Every year my parents used to buy me one box of new Christmas balls to hang on our tree. Sometimes the box had four balls, sometimes six. The fir tree had to be real, and the only places where you could get one were the city market place or the fruit and veg shop, the *aprozar*. With only a few branches, they didn't make the best Christmas trees, but they used to make me so happy. Our trees were always taller than necessary, and my father used to cut some branches to make it fit in the only available space in the living room: on top of the cupboard, against the window, next to our paired phone. Eventually he moved the tree onto the floor, and we couldn't use our window for the whole Christmas period. After he had fitted the fairy lights to the tree, it was my turn to start decorating it. Back then we had only one bag of decorations, and mine was made from beautifully-coloured water lilies.

Every year the council set up a 'Children's Little City' in the city centre, with a massive tree in the middle, and an 'Old Freezing Man' inside. Sometimes they chose a different location; we had a beautiful park, called Crang, at the city gates with a big pond and a Liberty Style Architecture Villa inside. In the past it had belonged to a very rich family, but it had been turned into a restaurant with a beer garden. Nowadays we would call the 'Children's Little City' a Christmas market – but we were a communist country and we weren't allowed to celebrate Christmas, or at least we couldn't call it by its real religious name. But we all knew that the 'Old Freezing Man', who used to give away presents on 25th December each year, in reality was Father Christmas.

The regime couldn't forbid everything, especially regarding people's religion, but they set up a long list of rules in order to avoid religiosity. You weren't allowed to publicise or promote any religious occasion, such as Easter, Christmas or Saints' Days. Military staff weren't allowed to have priests in their homes. But before any important religious event, the Orthodox priests used to visit our apartments for purification and benediction, in exchange for a few lei. Whenever one of them knocked on our door, with a bunch of basil in one hand and holy water in the other, my mother had to whisper: 'Sorry, but you know.. my husband is in the military.' I'm not religious, but I respect any person who dedicates their life to trying to make other people's lives better, and to do the right things in life. That is a great purpose, if not the greatest, and I'm sure those people came to our home with only good intentions. It makes me feel a bit guilty now, to think that we used to send them away.

We waited excitedly for New Year's Eve, because that was the only evening during the year when we had non–stop television programmes. Usually the programmes ended at 10pm, but not that night, so I was allowed to watch television until I fell asleep, while my parents were celebrating with friends.

I loved watching TV, especially on Sundays during the winter, when I got back from ice skating. Skating was one of my favourite hobbies: the only outdoor ice rink was at the edge of town, next to the milk factory, and I used to walk the two kilometres there and back with my friends, or sometimes with my father. There was a bus, but you never knew how long you would have to wait for, in temperatures well below freezing. I began to ice skate on my own when I was five, when my father came home with a pair of size 2 skates. I was so happy that I put them on straight away, and, with my mother supervising from the kitchen window, I went to skate on the bumpy pavement in front of our building. I didn't fall over once. I was a tenacious and ambitious child, and my mother was very proud of me. Our neighbours were amazed, too.

Every Sunday morning I woke up early to be at the rink for 9am. It was the best time for children, as it wasn't so busy and there were no older kids. There were no real rules – you could skate in any direction and at any speed, so it could be dangerous too. But nothing could have stopped me from going there. When my father was watching me from behind the fence I was so happy to be able to show him my new moves. There was a kiosk, on the milk factory side, where they used to sell hot chocolate puddings for two lei. That was the best treat ever at the end of a happy skating session. My feet were frozen and wet by the time I got off the ice, and I remember a sort of relief when I could put my winter boots back on. Soggy, frozen, hands bent by the cold, a red nose and cheeks and my scarf full of icicles, I was the happiest kid in the world! I used to almost run back home, because at 11.30am began a children's programme on television that I was desperate not to miss.

I have only one memory of Easter, and that was in 1982, when I was living with my grandparents while my parents were in Africa for a few months. My grandmother lived on the fourth and last floor of building number 16, not far from my school. She was a very attentive and careful neighbour, and she knew everyone in the building. She was a good cook as well, and every time she baked or made a cake she used to share it with a few of them.

The custom was to wear something brand new on Easter Day, and I remember that she bought me this light orange cotton dress, with a zip at the front and a couple of creases on the skirt. In white socks and black shoes, I was ready to go to every flat in the building with plates full of food, accompanied by a glass of wine and a lighted candle, to remember the members of our family who had passed away. There is a Romanian Orthodox name for this tradition: *pomana*. The closest English word might be 'charity', but it doesn't quite have the same meaning. It is said that the deceased people to whom you dedicate this food will feel the flavour of it, and will be happy to receive it. More than that, they are expecting it on certain dates in the Orthodox calendar. It had to be a complete meal. On some occasions meat was compulsory, and there had to be a piece of cake and a glass of red or white wine, but never beer. The candle had to be lit, in order to light up the world of the people who had passed.

We started on the ground floor, where Mr and Mrs Nicolau lived. They were a very old couple. I like to think that they had a very happy marriage, and they were still very much in love. On the first floor, living in a tiny studio apartment, was Mamaia, an old single woman. She was 94 years old at the time. I never knew her name, but my grandmother used to call her Mamaia, which means granny in Romanian. She spent all her life crying for her only son, who died in the First World War. A portrait of him in a green military green uniform hung above her bed. She lost her husband as well as her son during that war, and since then had lived only with the memory of them.

On the second floor lived Mr Costica, a widower and a pensioner, who was always willing to help. He was a good man, so a portion of the *pomana* always went to him. On the third floor was Mrs. Dibu with her two teenage daughters. She was divorced, and worked for the Militia, which we now call the Police. On the third floor there was also a newly married couple. Both of them worked at the sugar factory, so they were a very precious connection. They used to bring us kilos of yellow sweets, little balls of sugar which sometimes were still warm. When they cooled down they became hard, and the only way to eat them was to suck on them or break them with your teeth. The sweets were made to be exported. The sugar factory was an important industry in our region, ensuring a lot of jobs for our community.

On the fourth floor there was a big gypsy family, the Botoacas. The mother worked as a cleaner at the hospital, and sometimes she came home with food under her skirt, 'borrowed' from the hospital kitchen. Once my grandmother was chatting in front of her door with a neighbour, Miss. Basil, while cooking a vegetable stew, when a very well-dressed man appeared. At first my grandmother thought was that she'd been caught by the police, so to save her conscience, instinctively she took the pan of stew from the hob and ran out of her door with it, saying: 'Hi, Mrs. Botoaca. Here, have some freshly made stew to give to your children for dinner. I know you're struggling to feed them.' The gypsy lady said thank you, and later on, when my grandmother met her in the corridor, she asked Mrs. Botoaca if she had been in trouble with the policeman, who had probably found out that she had been stealing food from the hospital. With a smile on her face, she told my grandmother: 'Oh that was Cirimindica, a friend of ours. He had just come to visit!' You can't imagine my grandmother's face, but she didn't say anything, and consoled herself that it would be a good *pomana* for the soul of her beloved father.

My grandmother used to borrow Mrs. Botoaca's children to queue for her when she needed to buy more milk, or cream, or eggs. They were always willing to help. We never knew exactly how many of them were living in the two-bed and one living room apartment. But my grandmother always gave a portion of her *pomana* to them.

Next door in a studio apartment was Miss Basil, who was cruelly judged for living out of wedlock with a man about 20 years younger than her. She was very ugly, with a broken nose and a face full of wrinkles, while he was tall, well-tanned, hard-working, and to some even good-looking. People used to say that she had used love potions on him to get him to fall in love with her. But I never listened to their accusations. Miss Basil was just a nice person, always polite and smiling.

After distributing the *pomana* on Easter morning to the whole neighbourhood, we spent the rest of the day eating lamb stew, celebrating with best meals ever and cracking boiled eggs to remember Christ's resurrection. That day was a very sunny spring Sunday and I remember how happy I was with my grandmother sharing those moments.

DRAGAICA

A positive thing about living in Buzău was that every summer there was a local festival called Dragaica. People came from the town and elsewhere to be part of it. Dragaica is a festival with roots in Greek and Roman mythology, and is celebrated every year between 12th and 24th June. The legend goes that the fairy Dragaica helps unmarried young ladies to find a husband. According to Roman mythology, the Dragaica's, or Sanziene, were considered to be evil fairies, who arrived on Earth from their Other World on the night of the 24th June, the night of Saint Giovanni Battista. If their arrival wasn't celebrated adequately, they would release bad forces of nature onto the Earth, such as hurricanes, thunder and hailstorms. Nobody ever thought to consider the

Buzău area as a magical place, but I think it had all the ingredients to be one – not just because of the fairies, but also the mysterious living rocks from Ulmet village, called *trovanti*. These huge rocks grow and move after it rains, and one rock, on Broscarului hill in the village Colti, is inscribed with indecipherable inscriptions.

I remember the Dragaica festival with happiness – especially the massive pop-up Summer Wonderland. It was a 15-minute walk from our home, over the railway track, after which you could start to smell the fried doughnuts, and hear the delirious music from the children's rides. At those sensations my heart started to beat faster, impatient to ride the Giant Octopus, the 'Tagada' flying saucer, the Ballerina, the swing chair carousel, and all the other scary rides. Every year there was at least one new ride to try, new magic shows, and different sweets and candyfloss. It was a street food festival as well, and you could smell from a distance the grilled *mici*, traditional Romanian street food made mince and spices served hot straight from the grill. perfect with mustard and a bottle of beer for the grown-ups, or a sugary Quik drink for us. My parents took me to Dragaica for the first time when I was three, and we went back at least twice each year ever after. All I remember from my first visits are what I have seen in photographs, but even in photos you can see that I was hooked. Every time I went through the gates of the theme park, a rush of happiness would come over me.

The hot doughnut kiosk was run by my grandmother's brother, Uncle Doru. During the festival he would come every day from the town of Ramnicu–Sarat 40 kilometres away to cook these wonderful treats. There was always a long queue in front of his kiosk, but as soon as he saw me, he let me jump the queue to serve me first. My privileges weren't always appreciated by everybody else.

I always came home with some souvenirs – coloured balloons and strange whistles and animal face masks. No-one ever promoted the festival, so only the people from Buzău and the surrounding area knew about it. It was rare to see people from outside our region there, and if you did, you could recognise them by their accent. We always saw familiar faces: from school, from workplaces, from the neighbourhood. We were all the guardians of this secret tradition.

SUMMER HOLIDAYS

Not all children my age could have a whole summer holiday away from home. We went to the seaside on the Black Sea coast as soon as my school summer holidays began at the start of June. When we got home, we went to my grandparents in the countryside; they were about 450 kilometres away, so we could only do it once a year. Occasionally, we explored places we hadn't been to before: Transylvania, Moldova, Bucovina and Banat.

Getting ready for the long trip was a sort of ritual, and all the neighbourhood was aware of it. My father started by preparing the car, opening all its doors, the boot, checking the wheel pressure, oil level, and the engine. Half of the boot was set aside for a couple of canisters of gasoline, which had been saved from the last few months' rations. Gasoline was less expensive than petrol.

With the car full of suitcases, a camping tent, food supplies, sun loungers and inflatables, we were ready for our summer vacation. With no advanced bookings, and no specific location in mind, we were always ready for an adventure. We would always end up next to a wide, sandy beach in one of the tourist destinations on the shores of the savage Black Sea. My father was the one with the most adventurous spirit, and I am very fortunate to have taken after him. Leave me in the middle of a forest with just my handbag and I will survive. Well, not only survive, I will probably build a treehouse and stay there forever!

The only unhappy person was my mother. She was the housekeeper even when she was on holiday. It made her depressed to bring with her our own pans and frying oil. I understand how she felt. To her, going on holiday meant going to a hotel where somebody else cleaned the room and did the cooking. Her dream holiday didn't involve buying fruit and veg, or spending all day cooking and camping. We used to spend nine or ten hours under the hot sun every day, with no parasol, just a white bed sheet laid out on the sand.

We always chose a spot on the beach close to the nudist area. This wasn't because we were especially keen to see naked people, but because here the Polish women – the ones who drove through our neighbourhood in their Fiat 126 cars on their way to the seaside, and threw sweets from their windows – ran a sort of black market from their part of the beach. In exchange for our Romanian lei, the Polish ladies sold us flip-flops, gold and silver belts, trendy coloured tights, chewing gum, sweets, bars of soap (the popular Fa and Rexona), food seasoning, cigarettes, sunglasses, plastic bracelets, hair accessories, lipstick, make-up, toothpaste, and many other items, which were produced with a flourish from their massive Mary Poppins handbags. All these items piqued our interest of course, as they couldn't be found in our shops. They were quite expensive, so it was with their profits that the Poles paid for their holidays in Romania. It was the only way they could change their money into our currency.

There were no services on the beach, like toilets or showers, but every hundred metres there was a cloud of smoke, a BBQ area, which we called the *brasserie.* Here the traditional *mici* were grilled and served with bread, mustard, beer and Pepsi. The queue was usually about an hour's wait, so before lunchtime my father would join the line for the most delicious food you could picnic with on the beach.

Nobody brought a towel to lie on – we didn't know that you could use a towel for the beach – so everybody lay on their bed sheets or blankets; the same ones we put on our beds and sofas at home. My mother always brought our best white double sheet, proud of her housekeeping skills.

We got on the beach about 8am to secure the best spot, not far from the sea. And although it was very hot all day, we would stay there until sunset. In Romanian we call people with nice suntans *bronzati,* which means those with bronze-coloured skin. In a perfect example of our lack of creativity (and zero interest in marketing), the only available suntan cream was a thick, sticky lotion called Bronzol. All Bronzol did was get you tanned quicker; it didn't protect your skin from the sun at all. I think frying oil would have given us the same result – or maybe even a better one, as the molecules in oil would have warmed up faster. Some people used beer as suntan cream, which gave them a sort of bitter smell. But we preferred the smell of Bronzol, even though we would all be burned after a couple of days.

There was another reason I loved to go to the seaside. My mother's cousin, Claudia, was a hotel receptionist, and every year we used to visit her in the hotel where she worked. She was a beautiful woman, with dark, wavy hair, big green eyes, a perfect body and perfect make-up, and always with long nails and high heels. On top of that she spoke three languages fluently. Every time we came to see her she was talking to someone in English, French or German. The hotels were mostly for foreigners – French, Germans from the Democratic (not the Federal) Republic of Germany, Belgians,

and some Americans. The Polish were not as well-off, so they used to stay at our camping sites. Romanians could also book their holiday through the National Travel Agency called ONT (National Office of Tourism) which had its regional offices called OJT (Regional Tourism Office), while the university students could book their discounted holidays through BTT (The Youth Tourism Office). It was a very simple institution, but we preferred to save on the fees, so 'DIY' holidays were about 90% of the market. Claudia knew how to treat her guests well, especially the foreign ones. She would send the housekeeper to their rooms twice a day with fresh towels, a bottle of sparkling water, more toiletries, and in return they would leave her little presents, like chocolate, cigarettes, perfumes and lipstick. When she became a hotel manager, I decided that it was the career that I wanted, too. I wanted to become like her, and study to have that dream job as a hotel manager.

HOLIDAYS WITH MY GRANDPARENTS

After the seaside break, which was usually for about a week or 10 days, we went to my grandparents, my father's parents, in Oltenia, 450 kilometres west of Buzău. It was an exhausting journey in our carrot-coloured Dacia 1300, with no air conditioning, and every centilitre of gasoline counted.

For me the journey was divided in four parts: from Buzău to Bucharest (about 100 kilometres on a busy two-lane road); from Bucharest to Pite□ti (another 100 kilometres of boring road, the country's only motorway); then another 130 kilometres from Pite□ti to Craiova (another two-lane road); then the last bit from Craiova to Piscoiu, 70 kilometres of country lanes, of which about 40 were unpaved road, which sometimes complicated the journey. The village of Piscoiu was the last one of a series of villages, lined up like rosary beads along a long valley between the hills. The road ended there, and my grandparents' house was almost the last one, at the very foot of the Carpathians. There was no traffic, no noise, no pollution. We were surrounded by century-old oak trees; there were no bars, no shops, just nature and its sounds, which, paradoxically, were sometimes interrupted by the noise of commercial airplanes, because the village was below an air corridor.

It was like a corner of Heaven – but I wasn't as enthusiastic about it as I wanted to be. After a day or two my skin was covered in red itchy blotches: I was allergic to something, but we didn't know what. Every year we tried different medicines and remedies, and saw a doctor. My grandmother treated the blotches with plants picked from the forest, with infusions, with special oils that she made, or with apple vinegar. But it was all in vain: both traditional and alternative medicine failed, and I just ended up with drinking litres of bitter *Clorocalcin* and taking heaps of *Feniramin* pills, which only made me drowsy. My nights were a nightmare. My cousin Diana, to check whether the latest cure had had any effect, used to circle every bubble on my skin with a pen. These hives ruined all my holidays with my grandparents. Over forty years later, whenever I go to that village the blotches come back. It is the only place on Earth where this happens to me.

It was impossible to 'cooperate' that remote corner of the country. The communists weren't able to grab the land and possessions from the villagers of Piscoiu, so it became a sort of communism-free village. My grandfather managed to keep his large estate in the village, which covered part of the forests and hills. They had a plum orchard, apple trees, grape vines, corn plantations, beehives, vegetable gardens, and a farm with at least two cows, pigs, chickens, geese, ducks, turkeys, a puppy and a cat. Usually the cooperatives would take everything from the village folk, and would let them keep only a fraction of what they had produced. Owning their own land meant that my grandparents could keep all their produce for themselves. But not being under the communists' control had its disadvantages too. There were no paved streets, and I remember that my grandfather built the stone road in front of their house with his own hands, over many years, by unloading trucks full of stones every time he was able to bring one from the city.

Electricity arrived in the village at the end of the sixties, and my grandparents bought their first black and white TV set at the end of the seventies. The council was about 15 kilometres away, and there you could use a landline telephone for emergencies. First you had to make a request to use the phone, then you waited for hours to be connected. Next to the council was the Militia (Police) office, a general shop, and the dreaded agricultural production cooperative – CAP, the institution in charge of collecting the produce that the village folk had grown. It was here that my father's sister Maria lived. She was the only veterinarian in the village, and lived with my four cousins and her husband, Mihai, who was the head teacher of the local school. He taught mathematics as well. Diana was the youngest of my cousins, about two years younger than me, and my favourite one to play with. With her I took the turkeys, ducks and geese and the mischievous pigs for a walk, whenever I convinced my auntie to let her spend a few days at our grandparents' house.

Our grandmother took us to pick blackberries, mushrooms and medicinal plants. She taught us all the names for these plants, and how to recognise them. August was the harvest period, and the end of the month was the perfect time to pick fruit from the trees. Our grandfather took us out at dawn on a cart with wooden wheels, pulled by the two cows, Joiana and *Floarea* (Flower) to collect plums from the other side of the hill. The plums were very important as they were the main ingredient in *tuica*, a very alcoholic drink, which was expensive (and much appreciated by the hard-working men of the village). The *tuica* could be made from any sort of fruit, and was often made with grapes, but the plum one was the best. Making this precious liquor was forbidden by law, even if it was only for your personal use only, so to cover their tracks, my grandparents also used the copper container that they made it in as a trough for their pigs. In the autumn their kitchen was transformed into a sort of Alchemist's lab, with steamy pipes delivering this elixir into other containers, drop by drop. My grandfather used to sit on a tiny three-legged chair in front of the equipment, and take the first well–deserved *toi* (traditional bottle-shaped glass, used especially in the Oltenia region, to drink *tuica* or *palinca*, the typical alcoholic home–made drinks) of freshly-made *tuica* or *rachiu*.

I loved going with our grandfather to collect the plums from the trees. He was both very funny, and very tough. He was a veteran of both the First and Second World Wars, and had also survived a frozen and hostile Russian winter, when he had walked – without boots – through the snow for hours after being released from a Gulag camp. Finally he made his way back home to *Piscoiu*. He didn't speak much, but he used to show us how to work: how to pick fruits from the branches without damaging the tree; how to respect nature, and how to recognise- birds by their calls. We became closer when once, while he was up a massive tree, by mistake he cut the branch he was sitting on, and fell off the tree onto the grass just in front of me and Diana. He was strong and he managed to land without breaking any bones. After a few seconds of silence and embarrassment we all started to laugh.

We used to come back home on the wooden cart pulled by *Joiana* and *Floarea* the cows, which was now heavy with fruits, ready to be fermented in big wooden barrels in the yard, where no-one could see. As he had a lot of land, my grandfather was always in need of working hands. The people from the village were always coming to his front gate, asking for a job for the day. They were happy to work in exchange for a bottle of the previous year's *tuica* or a bottle of wine. In this corner of Romania people were almost completely self-sufficient. They needed only very few things from the city, and we used to bring these to my grandparents whenever we would visit. We came with bread (a change from their polenta), seed oil or sunflower oil (instead of their lard), and sugar for them to use instead of honey. My grandmother preferred to receive flour instead of bread, so she could make her own bread in a special stone oven in their outdoor kitchen. Her bread was something special: in my life I have never tasted anything else like it. She used to make tiny loaves just for me. My mother used to bring her *Nechezol*, or Nescafe coffee when it was available.

Everything they ate, my grandparents produced themselves. And it was all organic: cheese, butter (that my grandmother taught me how to make), conserved meat, sausages, bacon, salami, honey, wax, jams and marmalades, and also home-made soaps and shampoo. They had a pond in the back garden full of fish too, but my grandfather lost it in a battle with his neighbour.

It was a perfect world. They didn't need much cash, so all the money my grandfather earned as a builder went straight under his mattress. With that money he bought my father his first Dacia 1300, the carrot-coloured one, in 1974. And he paid for all his four children's cars and weddings.

Each time we travelled home from my grandparents, the boot of our car was full of dead chickens and other unlucky birds, eggs, wine, *tuica*, honey, jams, cheese and butter, and all those items for which people used to queue for days to get their hands on. My father had many relatives in the village, and on our way home we had to stop quickly to say hello to all of them. They used to give us even more food, more bottles of home-made wine (which they were very proud of), more dead chickens, more sausages, more eggs… more everything. Everything ended up on the back seat next to me. There was twice as much food during the Christmas holidays, as every family used to raise and kill its own pig to eat. Because of the price and scarcity of fuel, we could only see my grandparents once a year, either for Christmas or in the summer holidays.

My favourite stop on the way home from the village was to

see my uncle Costica, my grandmother's brother. He was a tiny, very old man, with a long white beard and snowy hair, deep blue eyes, and crackly voice. He would wait for us in front of his traditional sculpted gate, propped up with a walking stick. From his larder he always used to give me a jar of his precious acacia honey, first giving me a taste of it from a teaspoon. When Uncle Costica passed away, it left a big void in my heart.

THE RIGHT CONNECTIONS

To get through life back then, everybody needed to have the right connections. The word is *pile* in Romanian, although it would take me many more pages to explain exactly what it means. Your *pile* were all your friends, friends of friends, and even their friends. Their help was always crucial, for getting food supplies, petrol, medicines, appointments with doctors and solicitors, as well as for gaining favour with politicians, the city council, forest guards and the police. Any connection was precious: the more *pile* you had, the more power you had. You were also more respected, and had fewer hassles.

We had a neighbour on the ground floor who worked at the garment factory. She gave us a few metres of coloured fabric to make bed sheets. One was yellow with scenes from Snow White on it, and another was white with giant red mushrooms and funny rabbits. My sofa bed looked like something from the movies. I'm sure this neighbour had her own *pile* at the factory gates. These fabrics, like the yellow sweets that our neighbours from the sugar factory gave us, were also made only for export. The only linens you could find in our shops had horrible patterns on them.

A family friend worked at the plastics factory. She brought us hundreds of plastic bags: white ones with 'I love NY' on them, with a red heart instead of the word 'love'. You may be able to guess where they were exported to. And there were little packaging bags with a chicken on them and instructions in Chinese and English, in which my mother used to freeze grilled aubergines in the winter. She also had a friend in the haberdashery shop, who told her when the Mohair balls or macramé thread were in stock again. Knitting and crocheting was her hobby and she used to spend hours making me dresses, jumpers, trousers and hats.

The right connections were also important when you needed to see a doctor. It was unthinkable to go to the doctor empty-handed. Sometimes they even told you what you needed to bring if you wanted them to examine you – the most in-demand gifts were cigarettes, soaps, Nescafe, chocolate, meat, cheese, eggs, or fresh fish. Any food item, foreign goods or cash was well received. I will never forget the image of an old woman queuing in front of me to see a doctor with a fabric handkerchief in her shaking hands, containing five or six eggs. I'm sure that there were doctors with enough dignity not to take gifts or money from their patients, but unfortunately I have no memory of them.

When my grandfather, my mother's father, was in need of an

aorta transplant, my family used their *pile* to have him seen by the right surgeon in Bucharest. While he was recovering, my grandmother had to fend off his nurses. They loved to receive foreign hand soaps like Fa and Rexona, or a pack of Kent, Marlboro or Dunhill cigarettes. It was an important hospital, so the medics' expectations were higher than elsewhere – but we had the right connections, and my grandfather went home safe and sound, after a 12-hour surgery and a month of recovery in the hospital. When all is said and done, our health is more important than anything. So if they had asked for diamonds in exchange for the right treatment for my grandfather, we would have found diamonds at any cost.

My dentist was a friend of my mother. I remember how nice she was with me every time I went to see her, despite the scary equipment that she used on me. It was always nice to have a connection who worked at the *alimentara*, the food shop. They let you jump the queue, and nobody would say a word. That was probably because everyone had their own connections at different shops. In unpleasant situations, connections were used as a retaliation against the person who was being unfair to you. Just saying the words 'Do you know who I am?' could inflict fear on your tormentor. It became like a Poker game, and taking a risk was never a good choice.

The highest risk was taken by those workers who smuggled products out of our factories with the help of their acquaintances – accomplice to their crimes, to which they were pushed by the system, and the lack of supplies in our shops. Some people risked their freedom, like the son of one of our neighbours, who spent two years in prison because he took home two brake pads from the auto parts factory. He was only 18 years old: too young to have the right connections at the factory gates.

Chapter 2

THE CONSENSUS FACTORY

MY KINDERGARTEN

My father was of the opinion that my mother should stay at home to take care of my education, so she was always a housewife. I never went to nursery, and if it wasn't for my stubbornness at three years old, she wouldn't have let me go to kindergarden either. But I was persistent. My daily efforts paid off, and eventually they decided to enroll me in a group for children of three or four years old.

The kindergarten was inside a Liberty building, which was now nationalised by the communists and given back to the people by expropriating the original owners, like my grandfather's house in Bucharest was. The house I went to kindergarten in had a lovely garden, with a few apple trees; this was our playground during our breaks, if we behaved well, and our teacher (*Tovarasha*[2]) let us go outside.

In my little handbag I was only allowed certain things, like a bottle of water (usually a recycled cough syrup bottle), a sandwich, and a square fabric napkin. Once I made the error of bringing in a beautiful red napkin with white flowers on it, which was from a foreign country. It was so unusual that Tovarasha didn't realise, as she was making her pre-lunch inspection, which it was made of paper, not fabric. But my best friend Monica told her about the red napkin, and I was put in detention for the rest of the day. The detention meant

---

[2] From *Tovarisch* - a Russian word meaning comrade, friend, colleague, or ally. It was often used by the Romanian communists.

standing up facing a corner, with your hands crossed behind your back. I remember looking at that corner for so long that I memorised all the cracks in the plaster. Thankfully Tovarasha didn't tell me to keep my hands in the air too, as she sometimes did to the children she made stand in the corner. But still, I was in tears for at least an hour. My best friend had betrayed me, and on top of that I couldn't go into the garden at break time on that lovely summer day.

Twice a week Tovarasha would also inspect our nails. We had two handkerchiefs in our uniform, a plain one and an embroidered one, and we had to put our hands on the nice one for Tovarasha to see how neat and clean our nails were. If they didn't meet with her approval then we were given a detention.

Despite all the rigid rules, I loved going to kindergarten. Sometimes we watched stories on slide projectors: the white fabric screen was so high on the wall that our necks were stiff for an hour afterwards. We had board games, building bricks, drawing books, and a lot of fun. In the winter, when there was snow outside, inside it was always warm. Being an old building, the heat came from an old brown ceramic wood stove.

My favourite memory is of rehearsing for a play, in the June at the end of each year. I always had the lead roles, and my mother used to sew me the most beautiful outfits. Once my outfit had a summer theme, once I was a pansy flower, once I was a snowdrop; and once I was a girl from the country, in a special traditional costume, and the famous Romanian blouse, called an *ie*. The traditional Romanian blouse is called 'ie' and it is one of Romania's most important pieces of folklore. With wide sleeves, traditional motifs, and natural colours, this blouse has inspired many fashion designers.

My worst memory from kindergarten is the outside toilet. I'm not sure if it was worse during the winter because of the cold, or in the summer because of the smell. The place was a hotbed of germs; I can't even call it a toilet. It was the size of a wardrobe, made of bricks, with two tiny rooms: one for the girls facing a fence, and the other for the boys, facing the garden. The massive hole underneath was almost never emptied. I don't need to describe how it felt and smelled. I only ever used it in emergencies, and it was so awful that some of us could only use the space in front of the doors.

TVR 1

The first Romanian television channel, TVR, was launched on 31 December 1956 using equipment from the Soviet Union. In 1957 it broadcast the first sporting event, a rugby game between Romania and England. One of its most popular programmes was about agriculture and life in the countryside; imaginatively, it was called Viata Satului ('Village's Life'). TVR could be watched almost throughout the country. I say almost, because in the remote countryside, in places like Piscoiu, there was no reception. But my uncle Mircea was inventive. He was an electrical engineer by profession, and built a 'flying saucer' aerial on the roof of my grandparents' old rustic house. When they bought their first black and white television set in 1976 they could watch some programmes, albeit with frequent interruptions.

In March 1962 they launched a second channel, TVR2. But this channel was only broadcast in Bucharest, Pite□ti and Bra□ov, so was out of reach to those of us who lived in the smaller cities. TVR2 was shut down in 1985 by Nicolae Ceau□escu, Romania's longstanding president.

TVR1 was on air from 4pm until 10.30pm from Monday to Friday, from 9am until 10.30pm on Saturdays (with a few hours' break in the afternoon) and from 8am until 10.30pm on Sundays. I always wished there could be more cartoons, not only *Mihaela*, a Romanian production, or *Lolek and Bolek*, a Polish cartoon that was shown just before 8pm every day. The only other programmes for children were shown for half an hour on Sunday mornings. These were mainly Romanian shows, like *Toate Panzele Sus* ('All Sails Up'), *Ciresarii* ('The Cherry Tree Guys'), *Pistruiatul* ('The Freckles') and *Racheta Alba* ('The White Rocket'), and they were really good, with great actors and directors. Other series were imported from the neighbouring communist countries – Czechoslovakia, Poland, Hungary or the German Democratic Republic – from whom we got programmes like 'Arabela' and 'Hunt.' On Sunday afternoons there was a programme called *Album Duminical* (Sunday Album), which was like our version of Laurel and Hardy, Benny Hill or You've Been Framed. Occasionally there were more cartoons, like Woody Woodpecker, Tom and Jerry, Fred and Barney in the Stone Age, Popeye the Sailor and Chilly Willy the Penguin. The 100 half-hour episodes of a Brazilian series called Isaura the Slave were also not to be missed...

Every Saturday evening from 1965 they aired a science programme called *Teleenciclopedia*, which was a source of knowledge for many Romanians. It included documentaries about nature, technology, art, health, the universe and much more, and I really looked forward to it. TVR also showed a movie on Saturday evenings, usually an American, French or Chinese one. The film was cancelled whenever there was an important political event to celebrate, like Ceaușescu going somewhere on an official visit, of the government delivering an important target. Then they showed some patriotic poetry reading or music instead.

On Tuesday evening we had some Romanian theatre, which was usually interesting to watch, and made a great impression on my childhood. The television lineup changed in 1982, during an official visit by the president of Pakistan, Muhammad Zia-ul-Haq. For the first time there was 'breaking news': the general's arrival ceremony and his departure were broadcast live from Otopeni, Bucharest's international airport. In 1985 they made drastic cuts to the amount of television that was broadcast. From then we were allowed only two hours of programmes a day, in the evenings, and a couple more on Sunday.

Being very inventive people, Romanians will always find a solution to any problem, even if it is more than a little eccentric. People could get around the two hours per day limit for television, as long as they lived close enough to our border with Bulgaria. Bulgarians, our neighbours to the south, had television all day. Their channels broadcast international dance contests, with beautiful dresses and music, as well as Russian and Bulgarian cartoons on a programme called *Za Deza Ta*. We just had to find a way to pick up these channels. There was no limit to our parents' creativity: on the roofs of our buildings were the most bizarre aerials you could ever imagine. They were made from frying pans, bicycle wheels, oven grills, aluminium basins of all sizes… any object of a size and shape that would catch these foreign channels. If you had a connection to the town's wire factory, your aerial would work much better. Some people put their aerials on their balconies instead of their roof, and people died from falling off; we would literally risk our lives for an extra couple of hours of TV. A friend of my father's fell from his second floor balcony, but, having been trained as a pilot, he managed to land on his feet, with only a rip in his jeans to show for it.

We would ask our friends: 'Do you *catch* the Bulgarians?' This was a source of pride for us, and a good subject for jokes too.

When I was seven my music teacher, Tovarash Tozeanu, put me forward to take part in a television programme over Christmas. We couldn't celebrate Christmas, so the way to hide the real meaning was to call it by a different name: 'winter festivities'. The whole programme was dedicated to our leaders, Tovarash Nicolae Ceaușescu and Tovarasha Elena Ceaușescu; to our Communist Party, to our socialist republic, and all our 'golden age of communism', as they used to call it. After weeks of rehearsals during and after school, sometimes practising for ten hours on end without a break for lunch, we were ready to record our performance at the House of Culture. The set was magical, depicting only a beautiful winter scene, with no religious symbols or Santa Claus. The stage was covered in artificial snow, generated by machines hanging from the ceiling, with a giant snowman in the centre. There were sleighs and white trees, lights of all colours, and microphones and speakers for me and my classmate Luana, for us to recite our patriotic poem by heart. After all that work, days of rehearsals, stress and tiredness, the time had finally come. We would be on TV on a Saturday evening before Christmas in the winter of 1979. To make sure that we would be able to watch the performance at home that evening, my father spent all day checking the position of the aerial, and the back valves on our black and white TV set, a precious wedding gift from my grandfather. I don't remember much of that evening – probably because I was too excited. But I do remember how afterwards I felt like a little celebrity as everybody had found out about my performance, and we received phone calls from all our friends and family for weeks.

ROMANIA AND GEOGRAPHY

I loved to dream about what life was like beyond our borders. I had learned a little from books, and from what people used to say about 'the Outside', which is what we used to call the rest of the world. For me, the Outside was limited to a few countries – Switzerland, France, Great Britain, Belgium, Italy, Spain, and the Federal Republic of Germany. These were the countries where our people would escape to, the very few of us who managed to get away from the Regime. I had also heard about the United States of America, Canada and Australia, but they just felt like a myth. I imagined them all very clean, shiny and sun-kissed. I imagined their countries full of shops, especially sweet shops, with beautiful window displays. I imagined people walking down the street looking happy, because they had no reason to be sad, like us. They were allowed to do things. They had beautiful clothes, like the ones I used to see in the Nekermann fashion magazine. And they could visit all those museums that I had only heard about at school. I used to associate these countries with the colours yellow and orange. That's how the Outside looked to me: unlimited happiness, and yellow and orange – the colours of freedom in my vision.

Meanwhile, Romania was closed off, as if we were trapped in a box. Our connection to the outside world was working millions of unpaid hours to produce Romanian goods for export. We weren't part of Europe, let alone the rest of the world. At school I saw on a map that geographically at least we were in Europe, but our teacher never mentioned us in the list of European countries. We may have had borders with European countries to the west and the Soviet Union to the east, but as far as our teacher was concerned, we were Romania and that was that. We never got answers to any of our questions. Years later, I realised why our poor teacher couldn't say anything about our place in the world. He knew about the Communist Bloc, and consequences that any careless words could have on his career – and his life.

BANK HOLIDAYS AND OTHER OCCASIONS

Every year, about a month before the school summer holidays, we began rehearsals for Romania's Liberation Day, which was on 23rd August. It was on that day that marked the historic destiny of Romania between 1945 and 1989. In August 1944 the fascist regime, under the leadership of Marshal Ion Antonescu, was defeated by King Mihai. The Monarchy returned, to all its previous power, and resisted until 1947, when King Mihai was forced to abdicate by the communists of the Romanian Working Party. Later he was exiled with his entire family.

The day of 23 August 1944, the insurrection against the fascists, actually brought about the beginning of a new and sad historical period, even if the promises made at the time were for happiness, prosperity and equalisation for all. From 1965 when Nicolae Ceau□escu has been elected at the guide of Socialist Party, as its general secretary, the period to follow was symbolically called the Golden Age of communism. "Upon his rise to power, Ceau□escu eased press censorship and openly condemned the Warshaw Pact invasion of Czechoslovakia in his speech on 21 August 1968, which resulted in a surge in popularity. The resulting period of stability was bried as his government soon became totalitarian and was considered the most repressive in the Eastern Bloc at the time. His secret police, the Securitate, was responsible for mass surveillance as well as sever repression and human rights abuses within the country, and controlled the mass media and press." (s. Wikipedia) The situation got worse especially towards the beginning of the '80s, but by now we were inside the powerful ideological indoctrination machine and without realising it, the initial infatuation had turned into a big weight that weighted more and more heavily on our lives.

From the little ones to the grown up ones, we were enrolled like in a small Army. Based on our age we were enrolled in a certain group each one with its name to be proudly called off. The Kindergarten children were enrolled as *Soimii Patriei* (The Falcons of The Homeland), the Primary school children were the *Pionierii Patriei* (The Pioneers of the Homeland), the High School students were called the UTC–isti as part of the Union of communist Youth Association which was including as well the University communist Students Association. The entire adult population had to join politically, paying their due annual fees, as members of the Romanian communist Party or other organisations coordinated by the same political powers as the Trade Unions called *Sindicate*.

There wasn't much choice, you had to be in in System to may get colleagues respect and eventually job promotions and people were too afraid to express their different opinions in case that happened.

On the occasion of any celebratory and commemorative event, everyone had to contribute with commitment to its success, in the name of communism and for communism.

The National Public Celebration was honoured with a massive parade, or better a mass parade displayed usually in the Stadium of each city around the country. The main tribunes were filled with politicians and communist Party representatives and other 'important' figures. As I anticipated earlier, we, children, were all 'invited' to start the rehearsal for the event in the playground every day during our break times and after school as well. Nobody was excluded and the school gates were patrolled continuously by the school teachers in order to avoid any escape. In the middle of the concrete stage, where usually we were celebrating the end of the year awards ceremony for the best school students, the PE teacher was organising each classroom in parallel lines like this we could follow the ballet he or she was creating for our school representation.

As any respectful totalitarian Regime, the personal life of each one of us was controlled by the State, and for this reason was compulsory to participate to these rehearsals and to be in the Stadium in the middle of our summer holidays. We were on duty and nobody was allowed to be absent and if that happened then your behaviour mark would've been lower than 10 out of 10 with important consequences for the university admission were you had to had 10 out of 10 for every year of your school education. So, in August, forced to endure almost tropical temperatures, we all went to the stadium to dance and sometimes faint, in the grip of fatigue and heat.

During the parade, the factory workers were displayed on the lateral tribunes. Imagine a modern Colosseum during the inaugural games, with the gallery for the Emperor, seating area for the public – the workers in our case and the arena full of lambs, sorry lions and ferocious animals. Well you get the idea. The workers duty was to wave in the air in a certain order coloured square boards or manifests to praise the Regime, like:

Long Life to the PCR (Romanian communist Party)

Long Life to *Tovarash* Nicolae Ceau□escu!

Long Life to the Socialist Republic of Romania!

Glory to the Golden Age!

Always Forward Good Workers!

Party, Ceau□escu, Romania!

No, to nuclear Bombs! (my favourite one)

Buzău, un–nuclearized city!

Party, Ceausecu, Peace!

All for the People!

Long life to PCR led by his general secretary, *tovarash* Nicolae Ceau□escu!

Our esteem and pride: Ceau□escu – Romania!

Were the same manifests you could read along every road or street. We didn't have publicity or promotional posters, we had these and massive paintings of the happy couple on the hills, buildings and other walls.

In the crescendo finale of the event, the placard–men formed the faces of the beloved president and his wife, in an explosion of applause and patriotic songs. It was a total madness!

Once, I remember, Ceau□escu intended to make a working visit, how they used to call it, in our city, Buzău. Ceau□escu's visits were always called working visit as they pretended to have a lucrative and educative scope only.
As nobody knew the exact itinerary of the presidential car, on a ray of one kilometre all the city streets were filled with us, children wearing our celebratory uniform of *Soimii and Pionierii Patriei.* Not to mention, that nobody knew as well the exact time when the presidential car supposed to pass, so we've been displayed at 1 metre distance one of each other, on the streets from early hours of the morning till late afternoon, standing up for hours with a flower in our hands, hoping to see the God of the Golden Age, the master of none, the idol of self – the tovarash of all tovarashes of the World.

Was just a very hot day, we were all tired and sweat, hungry and thirsty and of course no toilets provided. Few boys from my classroom peed on them and you could see the tears in their eyes. But there was again, no choice and no humanity allowed for teachers terrified as much as my class mates. There I felt the limits of the consternation, the grown-ups level of fear, the patience and the resignation of mere people which dignity was trampled with indifference.

Late in the afternoon, we heard from a distance, the voice of one of our school teachers, saying. 'They are coming! They are coming! All in line! Everybody smile and clap your hands! Clap your haaaands!'

The most expected moment of the day, I could finally see his face, I could smile to him. I was so excited! And here he is, in a black armoured car, with dark windows all up. Probably he was too tired to pull the window down after an intense and rich dinner with the city Mayor, after all that working visit in our city, because he remained behind the darkness of his car and I couldn't see him at all when he passed in front of me on the House of Protocol Street that day..

Once at home, tired and starved, I released the day tension in a long cry. That was my occasion to see him, our Almighty God, the one I even dedicated a poem which I still remember:

To *Tovarash* Nicolae Ceau□escu

I wish him long life, life without death,

To move our country forward,

On high and great peaks,

On new youth crests.

With me, and I was only 8 years old, the civic and patriotic education worked perfectly, because I was believing in the System, I was a good result of their indoctrination plan, I was a little passionate patriot. I was almost convinced myself that he could be a far far family member, as long as his origins were not so far from Piscoiu. Soon I've started to realise that something wasn't quite right and maybe the System wasn't as flourishing as I was thinking. And this happened when I've started to hear my parents whispering in the kitchen with their friends and I was promptly turned away together with our family friends children. The grown-ups used to tell us: 'Cover your ears' 'Go back to your room' 'Never have to talk with your friends about what we are talking inside our house' 'Speak quietly, the wall are having ears.' Sometimes they were talking about certain radio stations like The Voice of America or The Free Europe, radio stations that could only be picked during the night time on long frequencies, despite the untranslatable interferences. Those radio programmes were broadcast with so much courage by our compatriots who fled the Regime and emigrated to some Western European country or the United States of America.

PATRIOTIC WORK

Since I was in the Kindergarten I was used to make patriotic work in the parks, on the streets, cleaning and collecting the garbage. During the four years of Primary School, we used to go to pick medicinal herbs from the fields, chamomile, mouse tail and that was a nasty plant, with a hard and sharp stem but beautiful tiny white flowers on top. We never knew the end of that enormous amount of harvested plants that we deposit in the inner courtyard of the school.

Older we became, the amount of work was proportional too. Not anymore in the school nearby, they were outside the city, in the fields; not anymore during our school classes but before the beginning of the school term, they were proper working shifts, entire days of exhausting 9 or 10 hours working shifts, from Monday to Saturday.

In order to proof our patriotism, we had to give away about 2 weeks of our summer holidays and to renounce of another 2 weeks of the beginning of the school term for harvesting. It was always during the harvest time, September and sometimes part of October too. Every day of the week except Sundays, we had to be in the school yard by 7am in the morning, equipped with a bucket, a little knife and a packed lunch, ready to be piled up in the busses directed to the working fields and hills. For us, teens and teenagers was fun. Being all together, crowded next to each other was also a good occasion for the boys to steal some kiss on the cheek to the prettiest girls, to joke or to sing the kids working anthem, spread by the word of mouth all over the country, from South to North from East to West. I still remember the words and was more or less like this:

Green pepper leaf, ala dila dada,

Long life to our driver, ala dila dada,

Who bring us back, ala dila dada,

And never left us down, ala dila dada,

Long life to the car too, ala dila dada,

Which consumed the petrol, ala dila dada,

Long life to the engine too, ala dila dada

Who burned the carburettor, ala dila dada.

Despite the tiredness, the dirty hands, face and legs, the mud on the boots and some cut on our hands left by the knife while harvesting the grapes, on our way back to school in the afternoon, with in a boiling hot full of children bus, we were singing our souls out and we were louder than ever and the boys were playing almost violently the blind fly game. The rule was that one person had to cover his eyes with one hand and display the other hand on a side of his body while one of the other people who were surrounded him, had to slap his hand. After the slap the person who received the slap had to guess who that person was.
The class nerds were the unlucky ones to lose the game usually, always under the hammer.

Some children had the privilege to may stay at home covered by a medical certificate, which most of the times was fake, issued by a doctor family friend or by their mother or father who were a doctor too. I wasn't so lucky so I couldn't avoid my daily work and I never missed a day. Above all we went to collect grapes for wine production, because ours was a hilly region full of vineyards, but with the years I've learned how to collect the apples, the strawberries, the potatoes, the beets, how to separate the rotten smelly onions from the good ones and how to browse the sharp corn cobs.

According to the Agricultural Production Cooperative where we were designated to work, the rules changed. Once we had to work in this cooperative to collect the Italian Grapes, those for consumption not for wine, those with the big grape, tasty and not easy to find in the fruit and veg shop. The rule was that we weren't allowed to eat them, so our teachers were like police officers, like our guards during the working hours. If it happened to see one of us eating them, they had to lower our behaviour vote and to jump the lunch break. We were working based on targets and only if the target was reached we could have the lunch break, so there wasn't much space and time for chats and play. The most pleasant work was in this cooperative where we had to collect apples. The director of that cooperative was also one of my family friends but not because of that the rule in his cooperative was that we were allowed to eat as much apples as we could. That was a fun and clean job, climbing the trees and eating apples straight from the source. I remember that the weather was great too and that place was picturesque.

The worst job was the onion one as we had to stay inside this warehouse where in the middle was a huge onion mountain. We had to form a circle around it and seating on the concrete floor, with naked hands to may fell the consistency of the bulb, we had to separate the good onions of the rotten ones. The smell was disgusting and a few of us vomit our stomach out. We had a lunch break but the ambient was insane and I could drink only water those days. Next door was the city cemetery and one day during the break I went there for a visit with my best classmate where she knew at least a third of the dead people. Not only, but she knew also stories about their lives, how they died, how many children they had and how well her grandmother who told her the stories, knew them.

That period was a nightmare for many of my classmates as for me as well. With the corn was different, even if left painful signs on our hands, at least we could seat on boxes and wasn't smelly. I had a pair of gloves but not as much protective as I expected, so my hands were covered in cuts and bruises.

To collect the beets was a feet job, the only way to do it using human resources and not the machines. The perfect timing to collect them was when the land was muddy, after a rainy day was just perfect. I broke about 3 pair of shoes kicking the beets to get them out of the ground.

The effort was paid off and at the end of the working period we were paid cash, the equivalent of a dollar per day more or less. The problem was, that most of the times, our form teacher decided to donate those money, our money, into the classroom found to buy chalk and cleaning products.

THE CLASS FUND AND RECYCLING

Was each classroom's duty to collect at the beginning of the year the money from each pupil, for the classroom saving fund. We had to deposit, and it was compulsory, about 10 or 15 lei, equivalent of 3 or 4 pounds, in order to may cover the costs of white and coloured chalk, the sponge, coloured paper for the art lessons, PVA, the lockers, the handles, the broken windows eventually, the cleaning products, the table cloth for the teacher's desk, the flower pot, the paintings to hang on the walls and the board games.

We had a school janitor in charge with all the cleaning of common areas except the classrooms which had to be cleaned every day by us at the end of the school classes. The classroom fund was useful also to buy the broom, the bucket and all the products for cleaning.

We were working in pairs, usually we were desk partners and the day we were on duty, we had to arrive earlier in the morning, preparing the class for the lesson, providing the white chalk, cleaning the blackboard, writing the date on the high right corner and filling the weather pattern of the day based on the information we had from the news on TV. We used to share the same classroom with the grown-ups from years 5, 6, 7 and 8 and we have to be sure that was everything in order from the previous form. We had half an hour at the end of our lessons to clean the room including mopping the floor.

Once per term was planned and organised a deep cleaning for our classroom and that was including windows cleaning, curtains washing and all other table cloths, walls decorating or covering the stains, doors and window frames painting. Having one of your parents volunteering for it was an honour. My mother never wanted to come so the maximum I could get was washing the teacher's desk cloth. Based on their skills and job titles, our parents were kindly asked by our teacher to help out and nobody could refuse her.

Our parents' job titles were very important mostly when we had to collect massive quantities of paper, bottles, plastic and iron. Yes, iron that natural element from the Mendeleev periodic table which was almost impossible to find unless you were as lucky as us to have Sorina as a classmate. Her father was an engineer at the Wire Factory and he helped us every year to reach our target of about 500 Kg per classroom. Every child had to bring to school 10 kilos of paper, 2 kilos of plastic, 20 glass bottles and 20 of iron. While the last one was sorted there was no excuse for the other materials and we had to carry all those weights to school by hands.

We were just walking every day to school, wasn't a habit for our parents to accompany us to school. We were trained how to cross the road and never change the way back home. Our parents used to come with us to school only on the first and last day of the school. In the first day to meet and greet the teacher with flowers and in the last day to participate at the end of the year awards.

To carry ten kilos of paper was a heavy job so my mother had to divide it in 2 packs of 5 kilos each, tied with a string, one for each hand plus the schoolbag on my shoulders. Luckily the school was only two hundred metres away and getting there in time took me about 20 minutes considering all the necessary stops on the way. To have access to your classroom you had to pass the weight scale. If the requested amount wasn't reached, even for a hundred grams, you risk to be sent home to find it and get few hours of absence in the register.

Our other important commitment was to feed the silk worms

with vine leaves. Huge sheets of paper were spread on the last free desks, at the back of the classroom and on a carpet of leaves we placed the abominable worms that would soon become precious silk bubbles. To tell the truth, those hairy worms made a little impression on me and the boys joked about putting them on us terrified girls who in panic screamed with fear.

MAGAZINES, BOOKS AND NEWSPAPERS

As well–groomed little patriots, once enrolled in school, we were obliged to subscribe to certain magazines. One was called Pogonici Hedgehog (*Arici Pogonici*) and was for the kindergarten kids and primary school too, another one was called The Falcons of the Homeland *(Soimii Patriei)* with loads of articles about the President visiting the schools around the country and about the patriotic works and finally was The Braves (*Cutezatorii*) magazine for the secondary school. Nobody used to read them and they end up in the 10 kilos piles of recycling paper. As a proof of the subscription we had to bring to school the receipt.

We knew that exist better magazines than those because our classmate Luana had her uncles escaped to France, in Paris and they sent her a magazine printed on glossy paper, with beautiful shiny colours called Pif. Only touching it during the class breaks was a privilege, we were all around her desk watching the stories of that naughty cat only by images as it was all in French language, of course.

Luana had not only the Pif magazines, she had beautiful pencils, rubbers with moving eyes, out of the world pencil case all *foreigners* or from the *Outside*. She had even a notebook with coloured pages inside and that was a wow notebook. Who could imagine such a thing?

We didn't used to read much the newspapers in my house, as they were 95% political but there was an interesting newspaper called The Sport of which you were allowed to subscribe only if you subscribed at The Spark (Scanteia) newspaper too which was only about politics. If you had one of those precious friend working in the newspaper shop, you could swap The Spark with The Youth Spark one which was containing crosswords too on the last pages.

A magazine that was never missing in my grandmother's house, was Almanahul Romania Literara, a book rather than a magazine, in terms of size and number of pages. Was a monthly magazine, printed in limited edition and in order to have it was better to know somebody in that shop. It spoke little of politics and most of the articles were very interesting and scholarly. The paper of it was rough, annoying to the touch, yellowish, and broke easily if you weren't careful. The binding was very poor as well but the content was a payoff.

PIANO LESSONS

After she sold a precious gold bracelet and put upside down the entire living room of our little apartment in block of building number 2, my mother made me a present in the summer of 1981: a 350 kilos wall standing Belarus piano. It was a Russian piece of work, with a bronze resonance plaque inside which made him a much valuable instrument. It was fantastic.

Three times a week, Mrs. Seminovich, this tiny old lady, Jewish by origins, was coming to our housed to teach me how to play my piano. She was always seating on my left hand side and sometimes she preferred to use her old piano books, with yellow pages and some of them deliberately stick together. Were those stick pages that awakened in me the curiosity to understand what they were hiding. I once go a peek on one called 'Oh Tannenbaum' which was an off limits song just because was a Christmas song.

Sometimes I went to her house because I lived very close. Often her husband would open the door for me, a tall and very thin gentleman, with his trembling hands and his face marked by deep and long wrinkles that made him look very sad. He was very kind and I admired him a lot as a great violinist and pianist as well. He taught piano and violin as well, but his students were at a much more elevated level than me, that I was just a beginner. As a custom and a sign of hospitality, I was always served with a glass of water and some of their best fruit jam in a fine china saucer, while I waited for my lesson to start. Their living room was full of books and antique objects, black and white photographs in silver frames carefully displayed on the top of the piano next to a seven arms Menorah. Those photographs attracted me as a magnet, was something about them, all those beautiful peak dresses hand embroidered, bows and headbands, family pictures with children my age more or less and their parents, all together with smiley faces.. Once Mrs. Seminovich told me when she surprised me watching them, that they were all her beloved family and they passed away all together in the same time not long long time ago, while a tear crossed her face.

After three years of private piano lessons, my parents decided to enroll me at the Popular Arts School to study with more consistency the piano. All the lessons were after school, and the school was hosted by the Arts Museum of the City building which was a representative architectural building of the 18th century. The museum was famous as well for at least two objects exposed: one was the biggest world amber stone found, a 3 kilos and a half one and the Hen with chicken made of gold dated IVth century B.C. found in that area in 1837 during excavation for a new Theology school. I had to cross those corridors every time I had my lessons and I had access for free. What a privilege!

Twice a week for about four years, that was my favourite extra curriculum activity and Mr. Xente, my piano teacher, was very proud of my progress.

Chapter 3

ANGOLA AND THE SIRIUS MISSION

ANGOLA

It was a sunny day during the spring time of 1980 when my father came home from work with a wonderful news. He was shortlisted with other 29 pilots and about 120 military staff to be part of a secret military mission in Angola called The Sirius Mission. The duration of it was for two years and before the departure date they had a long to do list in order to be trained properly and ready for the Third World reality. As one of the best pilots, his duty was to train the young Angolan recruits to fly an airplane and make them ready to go to war in the South of the African Continent.

For me, the most exciting part was the fact that he was allowed to bring his family as well during his permanence. I didn't know much about that country apart the fact that I was to point it on the map of Africa just under the Equator facing the Atlantic Ocean. As my father started to acknowledge facts about it, I knew that the ground was red and that was a very poor country. Being a poor country didn't make too much difference to me, I didn't know how to relate to poverty at that age, for me was great the idea to travel abroad, over the borders of our Country and on top of it by plane; I mean a passengers plane. I was used with the military ones, and happened in different occasions to visit my father's place of work, to introduce myself in the cockpit of an airplane and even to have a ride on the airplanes runway when the boss wasn't around. It was an opportunity to see what is outside our bubble of glass, I could see the Outside World.

The departure was scheduled for the beginning of January 1981 and my father start to visit for training the Air force Command Offices in Bucharest, almost weekly. He had to pass many physical assessments as well, and was subjected to a series of medical and psychological checkups. Every time he came back home with more and more details and information about that exotic country, which made me and my mother more impatient to go there.

They had to send via sea 3 months in advance, all the necessary to live there for the two long years. The instructions were very strict and the content of that massive 80 kilos wooden trunk was checked carefully before the collection in place. When I say the necessary, I'm not talking about clothes and toiletries, I'm talking about plates, glasses, cutlery, pans, building tools, cooker, lamps, curtains, flower, sugar, cornflower, salt and a lot of canned food. It looked like my father was ready to live in Uncle Tom's Cabin but it wasn't that the case. Well, was similar and soon you'll understand why. Building up the content of that truck took my father about 4 months as every week they came with new information about the allowed and necessary items to add. I still see that scary wooden trunk in the middle of our dining room, which was also my bedroom of a shape of a coffin, with the lid open ready to be filled up. And same as an old style coffin, my father nailed it all around to close before he send it to Bucharest.

He had to be trained to pilot a new type of airplane, those that they would find once there. So, for more than one month he stayed in Bucharest to learn the control panel of the BN2

Islander plane, a twin–engine piston manufactured also in Romania since 1969, upon permission of the original factory the British Britten– Normann Group.

He started to learn by himself the Portuguese language with the support of an old dictionary that he found in a Book shop and this was awkward because the Command Offices were thinking of all the other aspects connected with the security, politics, survival, health but not with the communication. Portuguese wasn't a popular language to learn as it was English, French, German or Russian which we had to learn in school, so with his tenacity, as soon as my father arrived in Angola he wrote word by word in blue ink, his own 200 pages dictionary, that he still has in the library at home. His work is been appreciated not only by his colleagues but also by his students.

We were aware that at the end of this mission, our financial situation would've been better than before. His pay doubled as he had his salary as usual in lei in Romania, paid monthly and he had a salary in American dollars of the same amount of the original one. All the dollars, were collected in an account by the Command Offices in order to be released on a piece of paper to my father at the end of each year of the mission. At the time was forbidden by law to possess and sort of foreign currency and only the tourists were allowed to have it and to use it in the Shop shops. In Bucharest there was a different shop where you could buy foreign items with a piece of paper like the one my father received and that was called Comturist. The principle was simple: only the people in possession of those pieces of paper were allowed to buy there, no cash. That shop was amazing, was full of foreign sweets, sweets, chocolate, chewing gum, original perfumes, stereos, speakers, recorders, audio tapes, coloured jumpers, trainers, beer, whiskey, coke, cigarettes, coffee beans, Nescafé and vertical freezers that nobody had even seen before.

THE 1981 HOLIDAY

After my father departure in January 1981, my mother and I started to get ready firstly mentally then physically to our departure in June that year. Few months after his arrival in Angola, my father managed to make an intercontinental phone call and to get in touch with us. Oh, my God! That was an extraordinary event and both, me and my mother were home that day. Talking to him considering the distance and the unknown world he was calling, gave us goose bumps.

The first thing he was telling us was that the ground was red everywhere and wasn't as hot as he expected. At the end of the day was a sub equatorial area with an uncharacteristically tropical climate due to the relief in the interior, the proximity of the Namibian desert and the cold Benguela Current flowing along the southern part of the coast. So, not so hot as someone could expect from an African Tropical country.

We had a call for the vaccine against malaria disease which was very diffuse in that area. In order to have the vaccine we went to Bucharest and with the occasion we got the appointment at The Airforce Commander to apply for a passport. We got our vaccines and with it a box with Clorochin pills to may start the prevention. We had to take one every Tuesday at a certain time.

We received our green passports only few days before our departure and those were the most important documents we ever had.

Our charter flight was scheduled in June from Otopeni Airport in Bucharest. After months of excitement we were ready for the adventure. We met many other wives and children at the designated meeting point in the airport and I was happy to see how many children we were there. We've started making friendships and we never been bothered by the hours of wait before our flight would take off. Everybody was happy, smiley, excited, polite and curious to grab information from the others they didn't have. You could hear them saying: 'My husband told me that, mine told me that..'

After 9 hours of flight, we landed finally in Luanda where after another few hours of wait we've been divided in groups and distributed in smaller planes for our final destination, Negage where was my father Military Base, about 400 km away in the middle of the country. Negage was formerly a Portuguese Military Base and was functional at least till 1976 when Angola gain its independence from Portugal under communists' rules. The reason that triggered the Mission Sirius was the South African Border War known also as the Namibian War of Independence, and sometimes denoted in South Africa as the Angola Bush War. Unaware of being in the middle of one of the longest conflicts of the century, unaware of the danger and in the dark of the real purpose of this mission, we lived it as the most exciting experience of our lives and as the holiday of the holidays.

The Romanians were allocated in three sort of housing structures in three different parts of the city: villas, flats and a hotel. You may imagine something that looks like them but no, they were far from your imagination. Remember the trunk with tools that my father had to send months before his arrival there? Well, now you may understand why they were needed. The organisers of the Mission, ensure that the buildings were supplied with water, electricity, windows and some essential furniture. And that was all. At the end of the day there was a war territory in a third World country where children still died of starvation or at birth. My father which was allocated in the hotel, found the walls of the room black because of somebody used to make a fire in the middle of the room to cook and probably to illuminate the ambient. There was a lot of DIY work to be done and not only: a lot of inventiveness was welcome. Now you have a better picture of this hotel which was in an advanced state of decay, abandoned and partially destroyed. The elevator was not working but was only a 4 floors building, so not an important disservice. We were living on the third floor while on top, which once was a restaurant, now was a space for the events. Our room was facing the front entrance and the main road that was heading to the city centre, and was a wide uphill street with high palm trees on both sides.

As soon as we get there in June 1981, after a long hug with

my father we had our first brain washing of does and don'ts. We could drink water only after was boiled and cooled down, we couldn't walk on the street on our own and the worst, we were not allowed to make friendships with the Angolan people or other foreigners as we weren't there alone. Over the road of the hotel was a mini jungle and you could easily see the banana trees with a lot of fruits pending in bunches, avocado trees and papaya trees. I knew only the bananas and later I found out how many sorts of bananas there are and I've learned there for the first time about the avocado and papaya fruits. The problem was that even if they were there for free and many we were not allowed to pick them from the trees because of the tiny green snakes, hidden in the bunches shaped as bananas. They were mortal and that word was enough to keep us kids away, well almost..

Once the military buses arrived with us from the airport, tens of African curious were there waiting for us. They were watching us as aliens, was their first time confrontation in their lives with white skin children and seeing them, almost naked, with no shoes and bumpy bellies on top of their tummies, skinny legs, white crusts in their heads and lots of flies around their dirty noises, made me realise how lucky I was that I was living in Romania. For the first time I felt like an outsider, like a Polish person or one of those French or German tourists visiting the Coast of our Black Sea. The little we had suddenly became a lot and this aroused in me a strong sense of confusion and pradoxaly sadness. They were so quiet, watching us from a distance, some of them hanging on their mother's arms, curious but shy in the same time. In my 9 years old mind, things became more and more complicated and gave rise to new questions that I only answered after so many years. I'll always remember those big wondering black eyes.

At least the food, for us of course, was abundant and was free as well. We had to buy only the bread and as we were used to, we had to queue for it. For us, who were living in the hotel, the bread was arriving every 2 days and was delivered in a service room at the ground floor and served from its window. Only we Romanians were allowed to buy it. Even if it was always hot, just out of the military kitchen oven, not always was of a great quality. When the flower was infested with tiny black cockroaches, they had to bake it like this, and we had to spot them and take them out with the fingers. Let's say that sometimes that bread was full of proteins. It was a bit awkward at the beginning, but with time we weren't bothered at all. As a result, I am not fussy with food and I think I would do quite well leaving isolated on an island.

Often, in front of our hotel, Angolan women with lovely hair patterns, carrying in their head big plastic basins with all sorts of products, like peanuts, green coffee grains or fruits, were waiting for our parents to exchange their products with socks, t shirts, shoes or soap. This exchange was called *trocu* and they never asked for money. Their hairstyles were beautiful, none alike and the braids were made by arranging themselves in a circle, sitting on the ground with the legs crossed, were true works of art. They were usually dressed only from the waist down and completely naked on the upper part of their body, for the delight of our fathers. Some wives, probably jealous or just to joke, in some *trocu* occasion, gave them coloured and transparent baby dolls, umbrellas and high heels shoes. As they liked to show off in the morning when our fathers set off by bus to work, imagine them recognising their wives night outfits and seeing all these beauties with perfect bodies, wearing umbrellas, baby dolls and high heels. What a perfect way to start the day for our fathers while our mothers were spying their reaction behind the curtains.

Not long after my arrival, yielding to my insistence, my father bought me a baby monkey with a long tail, macaque breed 'muito pequeno' as they said, which I called Micky. This old man, wanted for her only a couple of pairs of socks, a T–shirt and a shampoo. Was nothing compared with the joy he gave me with this naughty companion which I had for the whole summer holiday.

In our hotel only, we were about 15 children more or less my age and we used to play all together every day on the dusty hotel yard while the others, the Angolan children were watching us silently from the other side of the one metre fence. Despite the not socializing with them rule, sometimes the boys invited them to play football and they set up the two teams and the international game between Romania and Angola was sorted. Not sure who was winning, I only remember that they had no shoes and they were running like gazelles. Sometimes we asked them to build us toys like theirs: they were made of fish, beer or any other aluminium can or by cork' wood. They were absolutely amazing, made by perfection, detailed in any aspect and they were running too. Sometimes they came with the toy car after one week of work and they were negotiating the price in terms of chocolate bars and soap probably for their mothers.

Sometimes we saw these kids, on the other side of the hotel, where was the forest, queuing in front of a tree trunk. You might wonder what for, well we were also curious to find out what for they were waiting there for hours sometimes. One day we went there, next to them to unveil the mystery. The kid in front of the queue was sitting on his knees staring this hole on the bottom of the tree, next to one of its massive roots. They were hunting crickets, not any cricket, those were giant crickets with succulent fat and long legs. Once the beige creature was coming in the day light, with an impressive dexterity they catch it, snatch the legs and suck the content. What a pulpy delicacy! Once the operation was done the next kid in line was following, and so on.

The city market was an attraction for us too. Once in a while I was going there with my parents to buy fruit or coffee grains. Not one of my favourite places to visit to be honest, firstly because of the tremendous smell and secondly for the disgusting food they used to sell like rat skewers, fried cockroaches, crispy chips insects, raw meat of unknown animal origin with flies buzzing on top of it and all these naked women seating on the ground with no underwear and not bothered to show their nudity. Imagine a movie scene in a market before the French Revolution for example, with the only difference that all the food was displayed directly on sheets on the ground and sold by Africans.

In the city centre of Negage was a Catholic Church ran by a Mission of Italian Nouns. Inside the church there was a cinema room, furnished as in the times of Lumiere, with wooden chairs, white walls and this white screen on top of a wooden stage. Once a week, for a couple of kuanzas, you could watch a black and white movie or even two. I saw there most of the Luis Des Funes films and also the Totò old Italian movies, all in original language, subtitled in Portuguese language. Romanian same as French, Italian and Portuguese is a Latin language and that was really helpful. I couldn't understand all but I was laughing a lot. On the way back home, we had to walk all together in a group and each time I felt a certain fear.

On 20th of August that year, for their 10th wedding anniversary, my parents organised a small party in our hotel room. For the occasion, my father built with a pressure cooker, a hair fixing spray can and a brass pipe an original Alembic Pot and he made our traditional super alcoholic drink *Tuica*. Tuica, usually is made with prunes but he had to adapt it to bananas and papaya flavour. My father, after this, became famous for his exotic *tuica*.

At least one thing was sure: we never missed bananas and I tasted four sorts. There were the yellow ones, that we find in our supermarkets, the yellow ones a bit thinner and with black spots, very sweet and tasty, the red ones with the dark red skin and the pulp pink, crumbling and sugary and the very long ones, not sweet but perfect for cooking.

My father's *tuica* was very well known after that event, and he started a small private production for friends only. Wasn't easy to have alcohol and in order to have some local wine, once we broke the rules and with my father and other family friends we had this trip outside the city, guided by an Angolan friend, about seven kilometres away from the city in a place called En Baixo. We had no transport so we had to walk paying attention to all those Tatra lorries and Toyota cars which were driven by people with no license driver and no speed limits. This place was in the middle of the forest where grew special trees from which logs came a liquor similar to wine, called 'Malavu.' This special liquid was coming out through a sophisticated system made with bamboo canes and ropes, worthy of an engineer skills.

One of the African friends offered to give us a lift with his car if we were willing to buy some wine jugs in change of money. Was a good deal apparently, as we came back home by a fancy rusty red Toyota car.

ROMANIANS, RUSSIANS AND CUBANS

The job of my father was to teach the young Angolan men how to fly an airplane. As a flight instructor he had to prepare al the teaching materials for the class lessons and also for the practical ones. He had seven young Angolan men in his class and they were smart and enthusiastic to learn.

He knew all their names but nothing about their origins, their families and who guided them to start this carrier. He knew only that they had to be taught all the tricks of flying the airplane and make them ready to go in war.

The working week was of six days per week, from Monday till Saturday, same as in Romania and sometimes he had the right of an SRL, which was meaning Free Recovered Saturday, that was actually a Saturday off.

The Military Base was about 7 kilometres distance from the hotel; the military bus comes every morning at 7am to pick them up and it bring them back home at 4pm. We went there many times, especially for the events organised in occasion of a Bank holiday how was the National Celebration one on 23rd of August.

In that special occasion, all children had to put up a play or a variety show and be ready to present it on stage in front of everybody. This time, was a bit different, not as the rehearsals we used to have in Romania. Here was more fun and we were quite happy to participate. Everybody knew my singing and acting talents and as we had important Angolan Military guests seated in the first row, I had to learn a poetry in Portuguese language. The poetry was written by their deceased President Agostinho Neto which was not only a politician but also he was known as a poet, and we all had to sing the Angolan Anthem which was started with this phrase: 'Angola nunca mai esqueseremos' which translated means We'll never forget Angola, such a true affirmation. Despite the fact that a new president was elected, the dead former president, Neto was venerated and praised as a Saint for the revolutionary ideas, he also was the first president, having led the Popular Movement for the Liberation of Angola in the war of independence. He was the president of the Movimento Popular de Liberacao de Angola (MPLA), supported by Cubans even after the 1975 Independence proclamation. He died in Moscow in 1979 and since then his mega posters were everywhere on the streets, on top of the buildings, like Ceau□escu in Romania.

We organised a beautiful variety show, we sang, we danced traditional popular dances and this time without having to wear our ceremony school uniforms. The show was a massive success and we impressed the whole audience. The evening concluded with a Gala Dinner and a massive fire bonfire. The Angolan students sang for us their traditional music and I was impressed by their talents and the musicality and the rhythms of their songs. My father, after that evening, managed to find an audiocassette with Angolan music which I listened for many years remembering that atmosphere.

As we were in the middle of the Civil war, our enemies were the anti–communist forces called UNITA (National Union for the Total Independence of Angola) backed up by the United States. The UNITA rebels were very dangerous, and this was the main reason we had to be careful and to follow the rules. We were with the communists, with the MPLA movement and not alone in that mission. Cuba and Russia was there too and not far from where we were.

I didn't know about what exactly was going on there and I'm sure our mothers were unaware too, but they heard stories about children boys being kidnapped by the rebels like dogs from the streets, given them a food tin in hands, and sent to war down south.. They were whispering these stories as they were afraid to be heard somehow, even here at thousands of kilometres away from home where the walls had ears. They built up their own suppositions and they were thinking that probably we were in the middle of a conflict.

Not far from our hotel, there was a white building surrounded by high walls and barbed wire, with military armed guards at the gates. They had white skin as well, but different uniforms, they were the Russians in mission for 'scientific researches' about the soil morphology as my father told me.

On the other side of the city was another 'scientific centre' ran by Cubans armed with guns and machine guns. Apparently there was contact between us and them as sometimes my father gave me lovely yellow Cuban sweets.

MOM'S STOPOVER IN PARIS

In September 1981, my parents sent me home in Romania alone. I wasn't quite alone, as I was with the group of all other mothers, wives and children on their way back home to be ready for the beginning of the school term. In Bucharest, an auntie of mine, which was working within the airport was waiting for me and she was the one who brought me to my grandparents in Buzău. My mother decided to spend another three months with my father and she took the first charter flight available in December. That flight had to do a stopover in Paris on its way back to Romania and the good news was that the stopover was for 7 days and their stay was financially covered as well. She wasn't alone, she was accompanied by other 8 wives all happy for the good news. They had a training period before, as Paris was pure Occident, and could've been a massive temptation to emigrate once arrived there. A part the ordinary rules to not socialise at all, to pretend to not understand any language, and to not nominate Romania at all, they've been told that if they decided to not be there on the departure day from Paris, there were bad consequences for them and their families. First of all, the husband would've been sent home within 48 hours, with no job and no possibility to get a job ever. This was enough information for them and despite the sparkly luxurious Paris, and the high temptation to emigrate as for Political Asylum, all of them came back home at the end of the seven days.

After years, my mother confessed me that she was very tempted to not return. She had enough language knowledge to find the way and to build a new life as a refugee. The French Government at the time, was supporting people in her position, with shelters, food and jobs, and she wasn't afraid. She even made up a plan, based on which in a few years' time she could've started the difficult process through our Embassy to bring me there. I was happy to hear that I was the main reason for which she decided to come back. Joking every time she was mentioning it, she liked to say that she didn't want to destroy my father's career as well.

After a 12 hours flight, they landed at the noisy and chaotic Charles des Gaules Airport in Paris. First stop, Exchange Office where at least my mother exchanged all her nine hundred dollars and then in a Duty Free shop. Was their first time in an Occidental country and all were so excited that after the landing they forgot to pick up the suitcases from the baggage carousel and once out of the airport they couldn't get back and they had to declare all the baggage lost. They bought, all nine, identical rabbit fur coats, cause was very cold and looking all good, all being in their early thirties they were changed by a ballerinas group. My mother was speaking a bit of French and so other of them but they couldn't proof it, so they just had to pretend that they couldn't understand any language and this was the trigger for all the fun for them. Their suitcases miraculously were delivered the following day in the hotel where they were staying.

With her pockets full of dollars, my mother made crazy shopping, mostly all for me and they had the time of their lives dining in posh restaurants and watching French Variety shows.

She always liked to tell us the stories about her trip that she used to call 'Nine Romanians in Paris.' One of my favourite was when she and a couple of her friends, went to a supermarket to buy some food to eat in the hotel, which actually was a family owned Pension. The supermarket was full of food, tins and cans all colours, boxes with biscuits and all sorts of chocolate and sweets. When she was describing this place, I was dreaming with my eyes open. All that food in the same place, all that abundance and the lights and the publicity and people with full baskets. As they didn't want to spend money on food because they wanted to save them for shopping, they were looking to buy the cheapest products as well. So, her friend carried the basket with all this tins which labels were with pictures of nice cats and dogs. They were very cheap and they were looking so good as well. Once at the hotel, they asked permission to the receptionist to may eat in the small lounge all together. Permission granted they displayed nicely the food on the table, almost proud of how good looking were all those products, and started to empty the tins with cats and dogs in few plates given by the receptionist. He spotted just in time the tins and he knew that they were unaware of the fact that those tins actually where food for cats and dogs. He tried to explain them but as they were trained to not understand, the worried man started to bark and meow to make them understand that actually that food wasn't for humans. Even if they could understand few words of his French, whoever could've imagined that in a supermarket you could buy food for dogs and cats? We didn't have enough food for humans in our food shops, how on earth could those French words have made a sense? This was one of her stories that usually left all our friends with open mouth. These Occidentals were really strange on everybody's opinion.

She brought me two suitcases full with presents when she arrived home. And she was smelling so good, and she was so beautiful and happy. The bags were full with trousers for me, a couple of dresses, pencils, erasers with eyes, Peanuts pencil case, even better than Luana's, chocolate, sweets, binoculars with Louvre, Arc De Triomphe and Eiffel Tour images incorporated, keyrings and all sorts of other souvenirs.

For some of the slides I should have a special machine but I didn't have one, so I used to watch them against the sun light from the window of my bedroom. All those paintings, monuments, street views were magic and the people in some of them have all smiles on their faces. In my opinion they were so lucky.

I knew almost every detail of those slides and I just couldn't imagine that after 20 years I would have the possibility to visit Paris for real. I deliberately got lost on the streets of Montmartre.

THE 1982 HOLIDAY

As a result of my father's mission abroad, at school I had a sort of privileged treatment. Somehow the teachers were more polite with me and I felt more protected too.

I was a sort of nerd in my classroom and every year I received the first prize, usually few books and a nice certificate and my father had to make me the flower crown to wear for the occasion. We used to go in the military fields to pick all sorts of coloured flowers for my crown. He also taught me how to make them.

I was not only a nerd but I was also very competitive and I was working hard to get the maximum of votes. 10 out of the

10 was the maximum and my mother wouldn't accept me to return from school with a vote less than 8/10. Was her believe the fact that she was 'sacrificed' her carrier to be a housewife and to take care of my education. So my votes were like a recognition for her efforts, reason why she wouldn't accept a low vote from me. I was a bit terrified too and I remember once coming back home with my form teacher to explain her why in that occasion I got a 3/10 in German language.. I got that 3/10 because Liviu, one of the naughty boys of my classroom, in that period had a crush on me and he used to throw small balls of paper on my desk containing love messages. Nothing would stop him to do so during the German lesson and while I was distracted by him, the teacher, which was a very strict teacher, asked me something about what she was explaining in that moment and because I didn't know the answer she awarded me with the first and last 3/10 of my entire school experience.

A part of this unhappy episode, I was a very responsible child, always did my homework without being asked by my mother because I had a purpose to become 'somebody in life', as everybody used to say. My purpose was to go to the University. It was also the only way to have a secured working place in the future. Once the students finished their studies, was University's duty to assign them a job, based on their final results and of course, based on your 'right connections' and how full your pockets were. To get a job in the capital or in a big city you supposed to have excellent results and excellent connections too. The lower the results, further from the city centres the place of work, sometimes in lost villages in the middle of nowhere, where you could find the best doctors, for obvious reasons.

Since then I knew if I wanted to be like my auntie, a hotel manager, I had to study Economics, the only faculty appropriate for the hospitality industry at the time. There was a limited number of places available and usually about 20/25 students were fighting for one place, reason of which the exam was very tough.

The University subject became the leitmotiv of any of my discussion with my mother and almost a threat when she told me: 'You must study if you want to get to the University and become someone in life!'

In June of 1982 when I finished my year three, my father wasn't there to make me the flower crown, so my mother had to ask a florist to make one for me. I wasn't bothered much that year, because I was more excited to travel to my father in few days' time. That year was different, as I had to travel on my own with the group of wives and children because my mother already used her one time a year trip to Angola imposed by the contract, from February till May. Even on that occasion, her return flight had to stop over in Las Palmas; this time for 10 days, with other adventures to encounter.

It was a last minute decision of my mother to send me alone to visit my father and we kept it secret all time. I was dying to see his face once there.

This time the trip wasn't something completely new, I was on my second experience now and aware of most of the trip process. I had friends from the previous year, I knew most of the faces and I knew all about the flight, taking off, landing, seatbelts, and hostesses on board, movies and the food on board. But this time I knew also enough of Portuguese language to make friendship with the crew and with the Captain. The Captain of our airplane, Josè, was a creole handsome young man, probably from Guatemala same as the origin of the Airline Company, TAG. He was impressed with my language skills and once arrived in the proximity of Luanda at 3am in the night, he called and offered me the opportunity to seat in the cabin with him and the co–pilot to watch the magnificence of the Capital city from the sky. They offered me treats and fruit juice and I felt the luckiest kid in the plane. I had a once in a lifetime experience landing while seated in the cockpit of a Boeing 707, and due to this story every person in that plane knew my name as the daughter of Captain Andrei.

The transit flight to Negage was delayed and the small connection airplane took off about midday. Josè, knowing about the delay, was looking for me in the middle of the more than 200 people group but unfortunately he couldn't find me as I was embarked on the first flight. He bought me a present, chocolate, sweets and a nice silver pen from the Duty Free but he didn't have a chance to see me so he asked a women from our group to give it to me. This story arrived in everybody's ears and I was considered like a small star in our group.

When we landed in Negage, my father wasn't there to wait for me as he wasn't aware of my arrival. I wasn't worried as

I knew how to get home from there. I got the first military bus directed to my father's hotel. He was on the balcony watching the bus coming and you may imagine his excitement when he saw me. Everybody in the bus knew my story and for a moment everybody was waiting that moment almost as much as me. Everybody got emotional once my father came in a blink down the stairs and he embraced me.

That summer they organised a one day trip to Kalandula waterfalls, known in the past with the name of Duque de Braganca. Located in the Malaje Province, on the Northern side of the country, they were about 200 kilometres from Negage. With a fall of 104 metres, this is the second spectacular waterfall of Africa after Victoria Falls in Zambia. Away of other tourist attraction, in the middle of the rain forest which cover most part of the country, this was a hidden magic place.

We left the hotel early in the morning with three local buses rented from the local authorities for the occasion. The busses were those for local transport, not for long distance once, so imagine the wooden chairs, not comfortable at all and the doors that couldn't close properly. The red dust from the unpaved road was all inside so we had to cover nose and mouth with scarfs in order to allow breathing. After an hour of travelling, the air inside the bus was toxic and we couldn't see one to each other. Despite the low visibility I could see out of the window the dry landscape, no trees, and massive cracks in the red ground.

As soon as we found some trees we stopped for a break and

to calm down the dust in the bus. There was no vegetation, only these naked trees and these mounts of earth with strange shapes, about one metre high, perfect to hide from prying eyes. The short break was interrupted by the scream of Mrs Sarbu, the wife of the colonel Sarbu, who saw coming out from the red mounts, giant ants.

Oh, nothing to be afraid of. Just the killer African termites-excellent warriors, with teeth sharp as razors, nobody told us about. They were more worried about the political issues than the dangers of nature, so no training provided at all. In an instant, running and screaming like crazy, we were all safe back in our dusty buses. After a while the rain forest appeared and we arrived finally at our destination, surrounded by a unique scenario, framed by a lush and wild vegetation. To reach the waterfalls we had to walk in the middle of the forest for about 100 metres, on top of this concrete pipe, making noise with wooden sticks to keep away the snakes. The landscape at the end of this walk was magnificent and that trip was an adventure from start to end.

In September, at the end of our holiday, we stop over again in Luanda from where another Boeing 707 of the TAG airline company would take off with all of us on our 9 hours flight way back to Bucharest.

But something happened and not went as planned. Due to an internal revolt of the airport employees we were blocked in Luanda's airport for hours. We've been all pushed in an external area of the airport and all our suitcases opened and vandalized in search of coffee, statues of ebony and ivory, snakes and crocodiles skin and other exotic animals fur.. Not sure what exactly triggered the revolt but I was crossed because they confiscated me the four kilos of coffee I had in my baggage.

Piled up in this huge shed, with a heat of 35 degrees, with no water, no food, we wait there for many hours to take our flight. I remember we were looked after by armed guards and we had to ask their permit to go to the toilet. Sometimes the permit wasn't granted and I remember some women crying in despair while the guards were laughing on us.

As a child, this was the scene in front of my eyes, this was my evidence of the facts but apparently there was more than that, some violent facts as well which have been reported only years after the end of the mission.

END OF THE MISSION

In January 1983 my father finished the mission and after two long years, he came back home in Romania. On his way back home, they had a stop over as my mother but this time in Rome.

He didn't bring many souvenirs as my mother did and of course he didn't spend all his pocket money, also because his relationship with the money was different. He did bring me the museums slides, from Vatican and Colosseum which I could see only watching them against the light from my window because I didn't have the appropriate machine to project them on the wall. That was my first approach with the great art of Michelangelo and especially with his Pietà statue, unbelievably beautiful and perfect. Because of its accuracy I had doubts that was made of a block of marble, but it really was and I had the proof when I had the opportunity to visit San Peter years later.

He did bring me some strange sweets, black colour, not really my taste but I ate them for the simple reason they were from Italy and in my conception whatever came from abroad was good. Liquorish sweets are not really loved by kids at the end of the day, so I wouldn't blame myself. The most appreciated present from him was a jar of Nutella, the goddess potion, which I used to eat in very small amounts with the fear that could end quickly. It last for a couple of months and once finished I used the jar for many years as a pencil support.

For my mother he brought a Gioia magazine, wrapped in a thin plastic foil. Inside was a plastic bag with six golden buttons, same as those on the jumper worn by the lady on the cover. There was a golden necklace too which I loved to wear sometimes pretending that was made of real gold.

I looked after those buttons for about eight years till my mother found the right occasion to use them on my 18th birthday outfit.

The most important purchases made by my father in Rome were jewels: three gold chains with pendants representing our zodiac signs except the one from himself as he didn't find the Capricorn, he was satisfied with a similar one, the

Taurus, that he is still wearing. He also bought new wedding rings and other bracelets and rings for my mother which they sold later on to buy furniture for our new home.

THE GOLD

I must stop for a short explanation about the meaning of gold and jewellery and about their importance in those times. Showing off chains, bracelets and golden rings was a sign of wealth and the gold was the only valid investment. Some women worn few chains on their neck, different styles and sizes and as many as possible rings on their fingers with a horrible esthetical result. Gold talks was a favourite discussion subject and they used to extoll how many jewels they have, how many grams each, how much per gram they paid and from where they bought it.

The quality of gold was based on its origin. The gold coming from Soviet Union was a 14 karat gold not so precious and less expensive but they used to enrich the jewels with nice semiprecious red stones. The good gold, was coming from the Occident, was the 18 karat one and usually nicely worked. The absolute less expensive one was the gipsy's gold. Somehow they always had gold coin treasures called '*cocosei*' (roosters).

The most important quality of any sort of jewel was its weight. The details, the quality of the design were irrelevant. The first question about a jewel, from curious people, was 'how many grams weights?'

The smile was another way to show your wealth in some desperate and funny cases. Showing off the golden teeth, the most expensive material in dentistry at the time, was a real trend. Having a golden tooth or a golden bridge was the equivalent of an investment in stock exchange, of which of course we didn't have any knowledge. But these were valid investments as once somebody was in need of money for an emergency, selling a tooth was one of the options.

Thanks Universe in my family nobody was showing off the wealth through his or hers teeth. My mother had one on the back of her mouth, not very visible and she changed it as soon a different material was available, because she hated it as much as I did.

The gold was a secure investment in any case, reason my father invested almost all his dollars in chains and bracelets for my mother once he visited Rome during his flight stopover in Italy on his way back from Angola.

NEW PURCHASES

Once the euphoria of my father return passed, and given the opportunity to enhance economically our lives, my father activated to change our little apartment with a bigger and more comfortable one. He also changed the old red carrot Dacia car with a new white one paying it half in lei and half in dollars on paper through the Comturist shop in Bucharest. Like this almost all his savings during those two years of risky job, were gone. Anything left has been spend in a year time for bits and bobs bought from that shop where the account in dollars was opened.

At the end, aside the new white Dacia car, we had a new JVC stereo, a massive Persian rug, almost bigger than our living room as I remember they had to fold it for few centimetres in front of the library, and on request of our friends they bought many jumpers and joggers with gummy drawings and stickers. I had one too, yellow and black and because was the only colour combination I liked and the pattern in front I had to accept it few sizes bigger as my size wasn't available. For more than one year we had whiskey bottles, Martini, soaps, Brooklyn chewing gum, Toblerone chocolate, Tic Tac mints, coffee, peanuts, spray, perfumes and cigarettes as a perfect gift for a doctor or a necessary 'connection' in order to obtain a quicker service in exchange or a better treatment. They also bought a Moulinex food processor, with functions that they never discovered, far too many to be used in a small kitchen like ours. The masterpiece was a vertical Iberna freezer which solved many problems of our winter cupboard space. The only problem with it was the space to host the huge freezer. So it end up in my parents' bedroom. The legend about the freezer was telling that you may freeze any vegetable and it will just be the same once defrosted. My dream since I was little, was to have a watermelon, my favourite fruit, for my birthday in late October. My father, even if he imagined the outcome of the experiment, listened to my request and freeze a small watermelon in order to have it for my birthday. Was a good try and a massive disappointment for me when the watermelon became flat and watery once defrosted.

In 1983 the technology started to make big steps and I remember hearing voices about a video recorder. In my imagination was a sort of recorder with incorporated a 15 inches tv in the middle and once the audio cassette was in and running, I could see the singers in the telly. Well, that was the video player in my imagination, far from the reality of course and probably for this reason I was disappointed when my father bought this black flat machine to be connected to a modern TV, possibly not the black and white one that we had with lamps on the back. Then I discovered that even the cassettes were far different from the audio ones, much bigger and you could watch movies too, it was called VHS.

Even if we didn't have the right TV set to connect our video player, while waiting for a bigger home, my father bought a dozen of blank VHS in order to record movies on them. He had a friend, a prematurely retired military because of a car accident who forced him to live in a wheelchair for the rest of his life, which set up a sort of recording studio in his living room. He had three silver AKAI Tape Recorders standing on a long piece of furniture and many other audio players, equalizers and synthesizers to get the best result recording audio cassettes and now VHS. He was our music pusher and I have the belief that he was doing it illegally too and not because of tax purpose but because foreign music was not quite an item to show off. I'll be back on this later. Like this, for me visiting Mr. Donea, our music supplier, it was a sort of going abroad. I always loved the atmosphere in his house and all that technology and equipment in his living room. He was always up to date with any new technology available in our country, and the last music released and trendy abroad. We had a collection of about 100 audio cassettes at home, all Agfa, BASF and few Panasonic I remember. We always had music playing in my house thanks to him. Once the video players arrived on our market, he was the first person in Buzău to have the right equipment to record movies. Not sure how, but he managed to have the best movies ever and my mother's ambition was to buy at least one VHS movie a month. For me, there were only titles on the back of the boxes as we didn't have yet the right tv or appropriate equipment to watch them.

Chapter 4

FOR BETTER OR FOR WORSE

THE NEW APARTMENT

As now we could afford it, after my father returned from Angola in 1983, finally the moment to have a new and bigger apartment arrived. The one bedroom and living room apartment in the block of buildings number 2, became a little too small for our needs, so it was the right time to make the move. I was dreaming of a room all for myself, my mother was dreaming of a guest room and my father was dreaming for a dry cellar to store tools, wine and my mother's winter pickles.

Usually, the apartments didn't come with a cellar in the basement, but if you were lucky enough to live in a building with a dry basement and not invaded by water and mosquitos, you could build with your own means, your own cellar. A metallic door, two brick walls and a lamp usually attached without permission to the communal area electricity and the cellar was done and ready for use. As a cellar area wasn't foreseen in the drawings by the building architect, there was no staircase to connect the basement with the ground floor, so the only way to get down there was a flying ladder with rungs and very dangerous.

I loved the idea of having my own bedroom and a studio room as my mother used to call the extra room for guests. We could finally invite friends to come and stay over for short breaks, well not family as they usually auto–invite themselves to come and stay over, which was also good from my point of view only sometimes. As by our tradition, when somebody comes to your house it's compulsory to prepare the food for special occasions, like Christmas sometimes and treat them with the best service ever. It had to be something to talk about after their visit and my mother wanted always to leave the best impression.

Back on the mission of finding a bigger house this time, my father started the search within his colleagues at work about his intention to swap our small apartment, second comfort grade to a first comfort grade one. The quality of the apartments were divided in comfort classes. The lower the number of the comfort the higher the quality. So, passing from a comfort 2 to comfort 1 was an improvement in terms of quality. As the apartment was donated to him from the Military Forces, as it used to be, the only way to have a different one was to swap it with a colleague's one and eventually to pay cash or other products the difference for the comfort and the extra number of rooms. As a military enrolled in the Army Forces, my father wasn't allowed to buy properties or to own private properties as houses or apartments. The Government was providing them with housing for which they had to pay only the common building expenses, sewage, garbage collection and the utilities. In few months' time, my father heard of this colleague who was moving to Bucharest for a better job position and he was willing to leave his 3 bedroom, living room, 2 bathrooms, 1 balcony and 1 kitchen comfort one apartment as he was getting a new one in the Capital city. He had 2 options: to give it back to the Military Air Force offices in terms to be re-allocated by them or to find some-one, military of course, willing to have it and to get some extra cash for it too. For sure the second option was more intriguing so he accepted my fathers' offer and for some cash, few bottles of Whiskey and few cartons of Kent and Marlboro cigarettes the awesome apartment became ours.

It was located on the third floor of this building of four floors, was about five hundred metres away from our old flat but this one was right on the Boulevard Unirii, the main road of the city, a bonus in our opinion at the time. All the buildings were brand new and they just appeared after the earthquake of 1977 which was a good opportunity for the Government to demolish completely the old houses and to build this horrendous but modern buildings of 10 floors in the first line and 4 floors in the back of them. Ours was just in the middle of two tall buildings, reason we were almost considered to be in the first line as we had a street view too from all our bedrooms. The living room and the kitchen were facing the back of the building where the parking area was. Unfortunately the basement was only half dry so not ideal for my father's project, reason he gave up.

In the summer of 1983 we finally transferred into the new home. Brand new furniture for every room and a teen bedroom all for myself which I choose from few options available.

Light colour furniture was a trend at the time and for both my bedroom and my parents one, we choose beige colours, mat for mine and silk for theirs. For the studio or guests room luckily we found an occasion: a beautiful cherry wood library made for exportation but refused by the CTC (the quality control authority) for some imperceptible reason. The truth is that the cherry wood furniture was part of a kitchen as by the label in German language on the back of it, but despite its designated use, for my mother was just perfect to display her porcelain statues and sets of wine glasses.

The living room was furnished with a massive library which covered an entire wall, a table with 6 chairs in the middle and a poster with a beach and a palm pending on a side was attached to one of the walls, which impressed every visitors we had since. I know it was a bit gimmicky but was something very unique and one of those crazy purchases in dollars made from the Comturist shop. My father decorated all the house with paper wall. For my bedroom I choose an orange paper wall and I had a funny poster too, but much smaller than the one in the living room.

The core of the house was the kitchen which was really big considering the sizes of the regular houses at the time. We could fit a table for 5 people in there which soon became also my desk for my homework due to the new restrictions imposed by the Government. We could fit not only a vertical nice fridge but also the freezer, which in the previous apartment was in my parents bedroom. On the top of the fridge my father placed a little telly and the atmosphere in that kitchen was just perfect, especially during the winter time.

The fact that my father was in a mission abroad for a couple of years, was like a positive add on his professional and private curriculum. As a reflection of it, was much easy to make new friends, connections with benefits and as a result his reputation was much better than in the past.

Despite the new and beautiful apartment, the beginning of the eighties signed the beginning of the worst period of our existence under the Ceau□escu dictatorship. A period that lasted, progressively worsening, until December 1989, a period which we managed to face with dignity and to overcome together with all our friends, relatives and acquaintances.

THE NEW SCHOOL

I studied for one term of my year 5 in my old school number 15 in Karl Marx Street. Then my mother, with the excuse of the new house decided to move me to a different school. This time the school was integrated in the High School, a prestigious school dedicated to philological and literature studies. There was a class for each year of our level of study, so one classroom for year 5, one for year 6, one for year 7 and one for year 8.

All our teachers were high school teachers so, was quite an honour to be taught by them. The level was a bit higher and so their expectations. The highs school, was named by the most important Romanian Romantic poet, novelist and journalist of the eighteenth century: Mihai Eminescu and was hosted in a beautiful Liberty architecture style building.

In any other school, the lessons for years 5 to 8 were hold

during the afternoon from Monday to Saturday. In this school, the advantage was that all the lessons were hold sometimes also during the morning time, which for me was a good thing. We started at 7.30am to be finished sometimes even seven hours later. Our time table was really busy and on top of it we used to have a big amount of homework. The school was quite far from my home and to get there usually took me half an hour of quick walk. Was fine when we had afternoon lessons, but a bit harder when I had to wake up at 6am for the morning shifts.

Soon, I was recognized for my artistic talents and I was always named to be in charge of the organisation of the events within the school. Any occasion was good to organise an event and we were all happy to stay in school after hours to rehears and to find the right folk and pop songs, poems, dancing and plays for the event. The school had a very elegant Amphitheatre with 250 seats, with a beautiful balcony unfortunately unusable since the earthquake of 1977 due to safety reasons. Perfect place for school events.

Was not only the school that I was in love with, was also the way to get to school which was a street, called the Street of Independence, very long, full with linden trees on both sides and private houses and villas. Was a really nice walk, especially during the spring time when the trees were blooming releasing the unique and special linden flowers perfume. There was the armoured villa of our city mayor too, that I could see twice a day on my way to and from school. Always guarded, with grey and tall gates, was impossible to see something inside. A couple of times I was able to see the gates opening, when a black Dacia with dark windows was entering into the property, but never in time to see what was hidden secretly there. There lived the untouchables!

I quickly established myself among the top of my class and soon I was awarded with the highest title of pioneer of the country, the one of Commander of the Unity, or better and less pretentious the responsible of year 5, year 6, year 7 and year 8. A blue ribbon was added on my uniform to consolidate and show off my title, of which I was really proud.

PIONEER OF THE COUNTRY

There was a very specific hierarchical order among the pioneers, exactly like the one among the military. Each classroom has about 30 or 35 alumni and was divided in 3 or 4 groups. Each group had a group commander awarded by a red ribbon on his left side of the chest and the entire class had a classroom commander awarded with a yellow ribbon. Only a group commander could be an assistant classroom commander and next to the red ribbon he had to wear a white ribbon as well. There was a school commander as well awarded with a dark blue ribbon and only a classroom commander could be a school commander assistant and next to the yellow ribbon he or she supposed to wear a light blue ribbon too.

As in the Army, we were like officers and soldiers. The

decorations, medals, badges and ribbons you had were just a sign of outstanding behaviour and results.

When I was in year eight I was elected the commander of my classroom and later on the day, when the school election had place, I was elected the commander of the school too. Was impossible to have both titles in the same time but that day I was so proud coming back home wearing the yellow and the blue ribbon together. Few days later, my classroom had to organise a new election as I had to honour the higher position.

My new 'political' role was very important and I had to take part in meetings with the teachers and school representatives almost every week. They also called me during lessons which was a trigger for my classroom colleagues to become jealous on me.

Every school term there were a reunion organised following precise rules, same in each school of the whole country. They were considered as very important ceremonies for the school and they had to be perfect.

During class reunion there was a precise ceremony to follow. The pioneers, divided in groups each with its own commander had to stand up in between the desks following the height order. In front of the blackboard, was standing the commander of the classroom. The two flag porters, one with the communist party flag and the other one with the country flag, had to stay on the sides while the trumpeter and the drummer had to stay still in front of the classroom till it was their time to play. The Form Teacher called 'diriginte' had the role of the instructor commander while in the primary classrooms this role belonged to the 'tovarash' teacher.

The classroom commander was initiating the ceremony:

'Classroom, align!'

'Pioneers, for the reception of flags, attention!'

Then she/he was asking: 'The group's report!'

'Groups, for the report step forward!'

The commander of each group was saying: 'The group number one, with a number of which twelve present, is ready to begin the activity.' And so on for each group.

Then the classroom commander was addressing towards the instructor commander: 'The commander of the classroom, pioneer Andrei Camelia reports the following...'

So we followed the agenda that could contain: problems related to undisciplined students the organisation of recycling, the teachers complains organisation of the internal works, and classroom saving founds collection and so on. Once the debates ended the pioneer commander of the classroom ordered:

'Classroom, for the flags report, attention!'

'Our activity has terminated!'

The meeting of the whole school or unity, which I never understood what that was for, which generally was a display of students in a 'U' shape, had place once per term. Every classroom was displayed in columns and in front of each classroom and the distance of two or three metres the commander of the classroom followed by the commander of each group. On the right side of each class was the place of two flag porters and next to them the commander instructor.

In the centre of the field was the place of the unity commander next to whom was the place of the commander instructor of the whole school as the head teacher on aside were displayed all the trumpeters and the drummers. Also there were the two flag porter guards and another four pioneers with another role to raise the flags of the school.

The ceremony was similar to the one followed in the classroom but in this occasion was invoked the 'belief of the pioneer' which I remember very well: 'for the glory of the people and the prosperity of the socialist Romania, for the cause of the party, forward!' Once these words were pronounced all the pioneers had to respond all together with a strong and penetrating voice: 'Always forward!'

It could seem weird but I repeated so many times this ceremony pioneer formulas that I have them impressed in my memory.

SCHOOLMATES AND TULIPS

Few of my class mates were living in Independence Street. One of them was Beatris. She was living in a beautiful modern house, with two floors, a wide drive in front and a big garden in the back. Her father was an international football referee and often he was working abroad. For this reason she had many things from 'abroad,' nice shoes, nice t–shirts, dresses, sweets, chocolate, sweets, pencils and pens, pen cases, erasers, school bags.. Well she loved to show them off and we were not only curious to see these alien items but also a bit jealous. We were friends and sometimes I was invited to play in her garden, to climb the cherry trees from the garage roof and to have girls talk about Dan, a handsome boy from year 9. He was living in the same area apparently, because sometimes happened to meet him during our long walks on Independence Street. We blushed every time we passed next to him and our heart rates were higher and higher. Probably he noticed because he was smiling with the corner of his mouth when he crossed our eyes even within the school.

Our suitors were mostly our classmates. To show their preferences for us, girls, in springtime, they used to hide tulips inside our desks, waiting patiently for our reaction once we found them in the attempt to fit the schoolbag in. I used to receive almost every day at least a tulip, and became a sort of competition between us, girls to see who will get more tulips by the end of the day. When the market was invaded by these beautiful and coloured flowers, the farmers/vendors, had to lower the price as the offer was very high. So they end up to be sold with a very competitive price, making them affordable for our classroom colleagues. The market was also conveniently located just next to our school and during the breaks the boys used to run to the market to buy more flowers for us. Were days when I get back home to my mom with seven or eight tulips. Our classmates gave us not only flowers, but also chocolates, sweets and bananas. They did not leave signed cards or other signals to be recognised, but we were still able to identify them: from the looks they threw at us and from the small pieces of paper torn from their notebooks with proper love declarations. They threw on our desks these paper bullets especially during the assessments. We had to hide them straight away from our teacher sight. Sometimes we got caught and the teacher was stopping any activity to read the content of the funny piece of paper, which leave few of us breathless and embarrassed, and all the rest of the classroom laughing.

During the breaks was no control from our teachers, and we girls were at risk of unexpected kisses on our cheek and the worst case scenario was finding ourselves with the skirt up, because they were curious to see our legs. When this happened, our form teacher, Geography teacher Dogaru was merciless with them. Despite the fact he was a great teacher, he was very strict with us and his hand was really heavy when it came to naughty boys behaviours. He had one glass eye which made him look much meaner than he really was and was also confusing to understand exactly the right direction he was pointing. To not get wrong, we stand all still in those moments.

I never was afraid of him. My passion for Geography which made of me an Olympian on National level later on, was one of the reasons, the other reason was my political position within the school. I was one of those untouchables in some way..

As a group of students, we had our quiet moments too during the breaks. You could find us in our classroom, all crammed on a desk, to play our favourite board games: TOMANAP or GO. We needed only a piece of paper for each of the two teams and some general knowledge to fill each column with names of countries, cities, seas, mountains, names, animals and plants all starting with the same alphabet letter decided at the beginning of each round. Only the quicker team could win. GO game was actually the board game everybody knows but we knew exists only on maths paper with dots strategically drawn by each team in order to gain more points. At that time, I never imagined that this was a proper game to be purchased in shops in some countries.

We played with a certain passion each time, and happened to not hear the bell ring at the end of the break and the teacher found us all crowded on somebody's desk, shouting and laughing. When this happened, we get punctually punished with a flash assessment.

Covaliu, one of our mates was a very talented cartoonist. During the breaks, we also played naval battle on paper. He was drawing the military ships, equipped with all sort of weapons and move by move the battle had place in one of the most spectacular scenarios. At the end of the battle, the conquered ship was wrapped in flames and clouds of smoke. I asked him to make some drawings for me. I brought him an empty notebook and he filled it with wonderful drawings for me. I was convinced that one day he will become famous and he did.

THE ORACLE, THE FACEBOOK'S FATHER

The Oracle was the key, was the answer of all our questions and the revealer of all our curiosities. Every student had to have one, especially by the end of year eight, before we went to the high school. What was the Oracle? Was a 100 or 200 pages notebook with the cover nicely decorated by each one in case the cover wasn't made of plastic. Was divided in 2 sections: the first section was the question's one and the second section was a memory that each colleague would leave you for the eternity.

Setting up the Oracle was subjective and was based on personal preferences and curiosities. Some questions were standard, like this the first page was asking firstly your name. Being the number one in somebody's Oracle was an honour, that place was usually reserved to best friends. Once you decided to give away the Oracle to somebody, it would build up and filled up with all the information you wanted to have. Usually the Oracle was borrowed to be filled for not longer than a week, like this your colleague had enough time to answer the questions and to leave an unforgettable and unique sign in it. After the first question, the second one was when they were born in order to find out the zodiac sign and eventually the compatibilities and the address to may send them cards when in holiday. They were followed by questions about favourite actors, movies, cars etc. Then was the space dedicated to more sophisticated questions based more on curiosity: questions about meaning of life, about love definition and perception, about first kiss, happiness, success meaning and more direct ones like: what's the boy/girl they fancy in their classroom? Who would they like to be with?

The second part of the Oracle was the fun part of it. They could have few pages to show you their gratitude, their admiration for you and sometimes their love. Those pages were an explosion of creativity. Colours, different materials, like buttons, flower petals, ribbons, sequins, glitter, hidden pockets, secret messages, photographs and coded boxes were all allowed. Was really exciting getting back the Oracle especially from those you were really interested or you had a crush on too. Starting with 'Stop! This is my page!' was almost a rule. Using poems to express feelings or name of songs was a way of perception for each one of us. Sometimes was a sort of sensorial journey when real perfume was used to feel the flavour while turning the page. Was the paper version of our Facebook. Oracle was static but was able to transmit messages, deeper feelings, thoughts and even flavours. For me was even more personal, real, sincere and realistically than the modern virtual solution and I still have it in my Time box with the best wishes ever like:

'As the deer wants fresh water from the spring, so I wish you happiness in the future' or

'A small fish came out of the Pacific Ocean, and on its tail it said I love you never forget me.'

WATER, GAS, LIGHT AND CANDLES

In the eighties, the water in our properties became more a luxury good than a primary one. In my neighbourhood, we had cold water every day based on a strict programme decided by the Water Plant of our area. We had two hours of water in the morning and one hour in the evening. Was different for the hot water as we had it only twice a week in certain days. Miraculously sometimes happened to have hot water even three times a week. If you were lucky enough to be at home and to discover the wonder! The voice of the quartier sounds in this case, same as for the *tacamuri* the turkey bones delivered in the always empty Butcher shop or for the cheese not allowed for kids on the back of the *Alimentara* shop. The impact was more or less the same and the voice was saying: 'We have hooooot wateeeer!' The news had the same importance as the 'Habemus Papam' phrase for the Catholics.

My mother, as a good housewife, was always ready to stock up on water needed for use in our home. The bath tub, which its primary use was almost forgotten was the first one to be filled with water. That was the water necessary for the toilet flush and for cleaning purpose. Then bowls, basins, buckets and bottles for cooking, drinking and kitchen use. Any recipient was good and useful. The operation of filling the recipients had to be done quick as you never know for how long the water wonder will last.

I always had long hair and I had to wash it two or three times a week. When I was lucky, I could use the bath tub filled with the warm not always hot, water from the Plant but most of the times my mother had to boil the water in the kitchen to may wash my hair while I was waiting half naked and with my hair wet in the bathroom for the water to be ready for rinsing. Not always the water schedule was working as planned and it happened to have boiling hot water only instead of cold one and later in the years we started being for few days in a row without any sort of water, and believe me, that was bad. This happened for a reason as we found out from a friend of a friend who was a manager in one of these Plants. Apparently each neighbourhood had an allocated quote to use within a certain period of time. If the water allocation wasn't done properly it happened to have these sort of gaps on its distribution and this explains it all and why once we've been without any drop of water for three days.

The situation in our Capital, was different. They had cold water in their houses every day and for the whole day, not only for few hours. In my dreams, that was a place I would have liked to live.

On gas matter we were lucky I can say. As in the block of buildings number two, even in this new one we had central heating and we were connected to a gas pipe in our kitchen for the hub and oven. The gas was distributed by the Gas Plant in this occasion. The difference with the water was that we had always gas in our pipes and that was our saving boat during the freezing winters. In other situations, where there was no city council gas supply, people had to use the gas tanks and to get them refilled was a nightmare. Firstly, you could have only one per household and secondly you could refilled it only once a month after waiting in a queue for many hours. This wasn't our problem but my grandmother's problem and I felt for her sometimes. The kitchen was the only warm room in the house thanks to our gas oven. Romania was rich in gas natural resources and it's price was very low. We could use it without limits within our houses. Not a healthy way to heat the properties but there was no alternative available. As the oven was almost always on during the cold months, my mother used to bake jacket potatoes and slices of unused bread giving the bread a second life. I loved the baked potatoes with butter and we found out a new recipe with sour cabbage juice, oil and pepper. Unfortunately that was the only jacket potato concept and our inspiration in terms of culinary creativity didn't went too far from there.

The heating system, or better the radiators were all connected to the hot water supply from the main Plant of our area. To protect the radiators of burst during the winter period, we had to cover them in blankets as babies. It happened to few of our neighbours and we were terrified of the effects and the damage that event created in their apartments. The water inside them freeze and because of its volume expanded, they literally burst with bad flood consequences before the issue was sorted.. We never experienced this scenario due to my mother diligence and care. Being flooded while the temperature in our apartment wasn't higher than 5 degrees sometimes wasn't in our plans. This is ok if you sleep in an Ice Hotel in Norway or Finland but that's a different story. I used to go to bed with a hat, heavy pyjamas and wool socks hand made by my grandmother from Piscoiu. I hated them, as I didn't like the feel of it, reason I developed an allergy later on and I can't wear any wool directly on my skin. My skin gets itchy and red once I touch the wool. To warm myself better, I used to keep my head under the duvet and to breathe intensely to warm up my cocoon. Only when the ambient was warm, I had the courage to create a tiny hole with the exterior to may breathe properly.

The school heating system was connected as well to the area Water Supplier Plant and things weren't much different from the ones we experienced at home. The school uniform was compulsory but despite the policy our teachers allowed us to wear during the lessons, gloves, hats and scarfs. We weren't allowed to wear jumpers on top of our uniforms but underneath we had layers and layers of clothes to keep us warm. For boys was a bit different as they could hid the jumpers under the school jackets as long as they weren't visible and didn't cover the pioneer red tie.

And even the cold was tolerated for the love of the country and its prosperity. We had with all costs, to pay the public debts and this was one of the prices to pay. Everybody had to pay it, no exceptions a part the politicians. The eighties were the years when Ceau☐escu invented Daciada a multi–sport competition held every two years in order to encourage the masses to practice sport. More than 6 million people were taking part. The goal was to make us stronger in order to face the cold. As children, we were studying in freezing cold schools, with gloves and no electricity and water supply here and then, but he had his words of comfort for us: 'Just add a jumper on top, and you'll be fine!'

The public illumination wasn't exempt of the electricity daily cuts which was another price to pay in order to save for the public debt. The wooden electricity poles, were replaced with the concrete ones in a short period of time, with the purpose to hold only the wires that feed the domestic properties only. So, no electricity on streets in the evening anymore. In essence, in a short period of time from the wise decision, the whole country becomes a big black hole on the night maps detected by the satellites.

They cut the light supply in all public institutions as well and this was in coincidence with the pick times of work, like during our lessons in schools. In our politicians' opinion, supplying electricity during the night time was considered only a waste. Why on Earth we could use the electricity during the night time? But Romanians inventiveness was useful in this situation as well and they start creating artworks to illuminate their houses. Thanks to my father's DIY skills and talent, we had a proper lamp in the kitchen, powered by an old red Tudor car battery. That light was much better than the candle's one which in a mix with the hob's gas would've had only a poisoned effect on us. My grandmother was using a smelly gas lantern for example. After a while she had to open the windows due to the black heavy smoke released by it.

Unfortunately my beautiful desk in my bedroom became only a books and pencils display. I couldn't use it for its designated purpose, because in my bedroom was freezing. The kitchen's table was my daily homework space.

The parents to drive kids to school or to accompany them wasn't a trend at all. We walked to school on our own, with some rules in place in order to avoid any unexpected event. Was challenging coming back to school after the afternoon lessons, when the days were short and was dark very early. We were organised to walk in groups back home with torches to may enlighten the way. I had to walk alone only for a hundred of metres to reach my building. The most challenging moment was getting to the third floor where I was living as the building's gates were always open with broken door glasses and there was always the risk to find a shadow in the dark or a strayed dog in search of a warmer place. My heart beating was so quick and sometimes I used to call my mother from outside to open the door while I was walking up the stairs.

While we were used to a sort of pattern with the water supply, the electricity was a complete chaos. You never know when exactly was happening and for how long. Sometimes was lasting for hours, sometimes only for thirty minutes then back for an hour and cut for few hours again. This lights game was happening even few times a day for the sake of our domestic appliances.. Once the light was back, you could hear the voice of joy of the whole neighbourhood. Was like a shout of joy for a goal in a World Cup Championship. In those moments we were all happy, we were celebrating all together something we all had in common and this was something that gave us the strength to go forward. We were all in the same boat.

During the lucky evenings of light supply, the first thought was to warm up the bedrooms with electric heaters. Of course we had them but there was a problem: they've been using too many kilowatts and there was the risk to overcome the limited usage we were allowed each month. Every kilowatt on top of the maximum usage would've cost us double. Not only. The electricity panel was at risk of black due to the over usage.

Despite the winter cold and long nights, the summer was more generous with us and the lack of electricity was less important..

BLOCK OF FLATS NO. 34

When we transferred in the new bigger apartment, we made straight away friendship with our neighbour from the second floor, just under our apartment. The Dragos Family was a lovely family. Mrs. Dragos was an Obstetrician and also Manager of the Obstetrician Department in the city Hospital and her husband was a Biology and Chemistry commuter teacher in Braila a city on the Danube Delta. Sometimes he managed to come home only during weekends due to the lack of petrol and the train bad connections. His family was from Braila so, staying over during the week time wasn't an issue for him in terms of finances.

They had two sons in a late age for our time costumes and usage: Bogdan and Sandu of three years old and four years old. I got very attached to them and I considered them as my little brothers as I was 12 more or less. We used to have a lot of fun together. Taking advantage on their young age and ingenuity I was organizing for them fake expeditions to North Pole for example during the hot days of summer while the thermometre temperature was above 38 degrees. In order to have the most realistically experience, I was dressing them with heavy winter clothes, bots, gloves, wool scarfs and furry hats and put them in my living room wardrobe in order to take off to the North Pole while The Winter of Vivaldi was playing on my vinyl record player. Unconsciously what I was doing was a sort of meditation and visualisation moment, because I was asking them to close their eyes and to imagine the whole trip from the take off to landing and all the environment that I was imagining for them to find there. I was actually activating their emotions and their brains through meditation to believe they were in a cold place, surrounded by polar bears, penguins and see seals. They were so much immersed in the moment that they could tell me details of the surroundings. I was always wondered why they never came out the wardrobe sweating, despite the winter clothes they were wearing, but I know today thanks to my hypnotherapy learnings, that our brain doesn't make the difference between reality and imagination, reason they felt the North Pole cold in the middle of the summer, and that makes me smile a lot when I'm thinking about.

As all the kids at their age, their mother was always struggling to make them finish their food or to eat certain fruits and veg. So I had to invent scary figures as Citanela, the monster who was eating naughty children, Miss Fitil, the nurse allways ready with the injection and Jujila the smelly tramp who simply hated the children. Any of these characters was actually me in disguise, and they appear when their presence it was necessary. I was using cushions, wigs, heavy makeup, tights on my face and different voices in order to not be recognized. It took me few minutes to go upstairs, in my house and get ready for the scary moment. Once I met a couple of teenage lovers which were kissing on the stairs between second and third floor. I scared the hell out of them. I know these are untraditional methods nowadays but for us was fun and for how wrong, was the right approach as having a slap from a mother. For the record, I had the last one from my mother when I was 20 years old..

They were slaps if I came home with an eight out of ten, if I got dirty on my dress while I was playing out with other children, if I was falling off my bicycle and came home with bleeding knees and simply when she was nervous or depressed for her reasons and she felt the need to discharge her negative energy accusing me of anything. In short, I got loads of slaps in my life and heavy ones all from my mother though. My father was always my escape island once he came back from work at 4pm. He was always defending me and he never slapped me. When I was 15, after she beat me good, while locked in my bedroom, I cut all my hair and I did it so bad that even the barber couldn't help much... That was the culture and many people used to say: 'Where you slap, they grow up!' I honestly have different views on children's education and I appreciate all the changes in our cultures since.

I'm closing these brackets here and I go back now on our childish jokes which were completely harmless. The two little brothers always behaved well after the bad guy departure and they always wanted to know where I was during the short interference, because I never was there to witness the unwanted apparition. They knew that 'the walls had ears' and the weird characters could hear their comments and their names invocation in case of emergency and misbehaviour.

But this was one of those phrases we started to hear often in that period: 'Shh, speak quietly as the walls have ears!'

We lived on the edge of endurance in those years and often the spirits of our parents went high, especially in front of a pint or a glass of wine. Mr. Dragos was a restless man with fiery temperament, a respectable intellectual and very smart too. I considered him very brave as well, because despite the ears of the walls, he was saying out loud his thoughts. From him I've learned about the discriminations of our people, the wrong politics, the despots, the injustices we had to endure. Every time we had an unexpected electricity cut he got on fire. He was crossed with everybody and his wife tried unsuccessfully to calm him down each time it happened. She was the opposite of him, very calm and calculated. She used to shut the kitchen door in the attempt to contain the sound and she was sending us, children, away to play in one of the bedrooms.

Nobody was trusting anybody and was very risky criticizing loud the Regime. Anyone could hear and told you off to the *Securitate* - The Romanian communist secret police, and you could receive an unexpected visit from 2 men with long grey coats inviting you to their offices for an interrogatory. You couldn't miss that appointment, would only worsened your position because if you got that invitation, actually in their offices they could beat you, torture you and release you with an ultimatum: 'we keep our eyes on you!'

Mr. Dragos trusted us and he was telling his heart out and his politics views in front of my parents. He was a revolutionary soul and he didn't like to live in fear. He could live in lack but not in fear. For him was unacceptable. He was often listening on the radio, on long length frequency, The Voice of America or The Free Europe programmes. These were stations founded by Romanians escaped from the Regime. They were covered by protection and fearless they could tell the truth about the manipulation of our country under the communists. Where we were blind they opened our eyes and create awareness within intellectuals, students and not only of our country. Quietly everybody knew about these stations and the audience was massive especially during the night time. Who knows, maybe this was the trigger for our politicians to consider useless the electricity supply during the night time..

Thanks to these heroes from abroad, we acknowledged about torture stories, unjustified imprisonments, stories of prosecution, stories of entire merch wagons fired before Christmas just because the parcels from the families living abroad could contain too much luxury items or better too much Occident flavours, stories of people tortured and buried in a forest somewhere near Timisoara city and many other horrendous stories.. I could hear only fragments of the radio programmes because listening from the other side of the wall through a glass wasn't so easy. I and the two little brothers had fun this way too.

We used to call each other 'neighbour,' not by our names and Mrs. Dragos was my favourite neighbour too. Because of her important job in the hospital, she received many gifts from her patients and because she had many she was happy to give me soaps to add on my collection box. My collection of soaps was carefully hidden on the back of my library next to the dark chocolate collection one in my bedroom in a doll box. I had about 15 sorts of different soaps and I was very proud of them.

When she had patients from the countryside, she was happy to get food, like fresh milk, eggs, meat, wine, spirits homemade and sometimes living creatures. When she got sour cream she was making us homemade ice cream based on a secret recipe. Was the best sour ice cream ever! Seeing her performances and all the gifts she received I've started to get confused on my future job and I started thinking that maybe becoming an obstetrician was a better option than the hotelier one. I've changed my mind as soon as I understood that my physics abilities weren't on top to may pass a very difficult admission exam for the Medicine Faculty. I was good in Chemistry and Biology but wasn't enough, so I renounced taking Medicine.

Bogdan loved to eat *parizer* a sort of pink giant hot dog with the diameter of about 10 centimetres. He knew as well that all the food we had on our tables was there thanks to the generosity of our Government. He was a cute chubby little boy and when he was hungry he asked his mother: 'Mom, when the Government will give us 'palizel' again? We also liked the untraceable bananas and they were often asking about having them. During the summer, I used to cheat them with cucumbers telling them that I had unripen green bananas at home. I pealed them with the knife to look better like a banana and happy they had real bananas, they ate them all despite of not being very convinced..

If few years before was still possible to buy after long queues oranges, mandarins and bananas before Christmas, now was almost impossible and this thanks to a decision of Elena Ceau□escu, the wife of our president who said that we could get used with all those luxury food. So they stopped the importation. Maybe for this reason I love the prohibited fruits so much that they are never missing from my home. She, as the first lady, had also a massive influence on our wellbeing. Once she made a mistake saying in public that we'll going to have certain products 'when poplar will make pears!' This affirmation was enough for the young students to hang pears in poplars over the night in the University centre of Bucharest. No newspaper talked about the event and the pears disappeared by miracle the next day. Same affirmation was made by her husband in during a meeting in Bistrita in March 1989, probably they loved it. He said in that occasion that 'Romania will get back to Capitalism when the poplar will make pears and not even then!' Same action was followed by the students in the University Quarter, but this time they manage to hang pears in a plastic tree which disappeared the following day by the Militia's hands which without any result made interrogatories for a long time after that event.

Our land was rich and would be wrong complaining now for the lack of fruit. We had all sorts of fruit in summer and autumn time. We were in lack of all the rest which was punctually designated for exportation, from animals, meat, oil, fabrics, shoes, grain, petrol, gas, wood, iron and derivatives, plastic and derivatives well almost everything was good for exportation. We were only children and the public debt was weighed on our little shoulders too.

CHERNOBYL: ONCE UPON A TIME

On 26th of April 1986 around one o'clock in the night, occurred the accident at the fourth reactor of the Cernobyl Pripyat, nuclear power plant, in Ukraine, near the border with Belarus, at the time republic of the Soviet Union. Till the following morning everyone was convinced that the reactor was still safe and sound, while the Russians only on 27th of April started to evacuate the area of the 'ghost city' trying to disguise the disaster. Gorbaciov, the president of the Soviet Union at the time, was informed about the event only on the 27th. On 28th of April the Swedish recorded an increase of 40 per cent of the radiations and evacuated one of their nuclear plants, thinking of an unexpected loose. On 29th of April, the TASS Russian News Agency, couldn't ignore anymore the tragic event, made finally the public announcement, categorizing it as a medium gravity event.

This is how things chronologically happened and how they were reported anywhere else outside my country.

We were ready to celebrate the 1st of May, the international day of workers around the world and we were all focused on that very important event, which for a communist is the apogee of celebration. All rehearsals of any sort of proletarian manifestation, commemorations and celebrations were in place and we were really busy with these important tasks. But something weird happened that year: the happy couple, *tovarash* and *tovarsha* Ceau□escu this time didn't show up in public to assist the manifestations as usual.

During that period, between the 28th of April and 2nd of May, my parents and I was on a short break holiday not far from Tulcea city, in the Danube Delta, just next to the border with URSS and we had, as anybody else, no clue of what was going on over the border. We were camping somewhere on the Delta, enjoying the 'fresh' air and the nature, fishing around, cooking outdoors, celebrating on our way the

National Event. We went to a traditional restaurant, known for cooking the best fish soup with water collected directly from the Danube, as the special ingredient. We had our lovely time, away of any rumours, radio or TV news, newspapers or other communication means. Only when we got home we started to hear a sort of agitation through the people. I can describe it as general psychosis based only on the news received from Free Europe and The Voice of America news and nothing official. Then the word of mouth made its itinerary through people who started to made their own interpretations and have visions about eventually the End of The World. My grandmother was convinced about it and she was invoking the Nostradamus premonitions. Was a complete chaos and every day the weight of incertitude was worsening the general mood.

We've been officially informed about the 'minor event' only on the 5th of May. This is how it was depicted by our media. As the event happened in a nuclear plant in a place called Cernobyl only about 400 miles away from our borders, we were advised to spend more time indoors instead of outdoors. And this was said once.

After almost 10 days after the accident, they started to give us at school, iodine tablets and they asked us to wash often our hands with a yellowish liquid. Among us, children, and I was 12 at the time, circulated the most idle rumours about radiation and its effects like: if you've placed a spoon on your chest and that was not falling off, you could be irradiated and be dead in few days time.

My father had to spray the city with a yellow substance, daily with his aeroplane. If you were under his ray of action and yellow droplets fell on your clothes, well that was the end of your outfit. Only the scissors could sort out the issue.

For few months we had to eat only canned food and we had to consume a lot of powdered milk.

FROM BLACK AND WHITE TO.. TELECOLOUR

Those days, we didn't talk only about radiations at school. We were talking about the Telecolor as well, or rather the coloured television. Till then, you could see movie in colours only at the cinema as we had only black and white television at home. But now, you could add your name on a long waiting list in the appliances shop, in order to buy a Telecolor. They supplied only few every months, and the risk was to be on the waiting list for an entire year. But we had our connections and by coincidence our third floor neighbour from the previous apartment, was working as a shop assistant in the shop where our name was on the list.

Since we heard about the possibility of having a television who could reproduce colours in our home, my father activated himself to find the trended substitute which was a coloured glass screen to be placed in front of the main screen of our black and white poor television with the intent to see some colours. Well, the outcome wasn't great as you can imagine but in exchange was recommended by the optician.

Instead of black, white and grey shades you could see yellow shades despite the fact that the screen was painted with colours of the rainbow. It has its yellow effect indeed.

One day, during our lesson of Contemporary History, our very strict teacher, *Tovaras* Dumitru asked us a strange question. I wasn't one of his favourite pupils and I always thought he was hated me, at least since he tried to flirt without results with my mother during a parents meeting. Since then he choose to revenge on her by punishing me. I was terrified by him and always shaking when he interrogated me. This time, after he called the register, he said: 'Stand up all of you who has a Telecolor at home!'

All of us were petrified for a moment waiting to see who will answer the strange call. The only one standing up, challenging us with her blue big eyes, almost saying 'you losers!,' was Beatris, my friend. Not sure how other felt about it, but I felt so humiliated that I went back home with tears in my eyes and for a while I refused to go to play in my friend's garden and to climb on her garage roof to play.

I wished so much that television that I created a chart to annotate each day passed from the order day. I made a countdown from 365 days, worst case scenario. Having a coloured TV was a reason of pride, especially within the kids at school. Was a sign of wealth or of having socially or politically important parents. Short long story: you were considered a privileged.

Six months more or less after that unforgettable 'contemporary History lesson,' exceeding any expectation, the new TV set arrived and replaced the old and outdated one. Shamelessly was the merit of our neighbour who helped us to skip the queue in front of us and, after the red phone, we had the second wonder in the house: the modern Telecolor.

Finally with the new modern and advanced technology purchase, we could use our video player and we could see all my mother's VHS movie collection, which was guarded carefully in a cardboard box in the wardrobe. She was thinking of me as well, and she ordered from Mr. Donea, our movie and music pusher, entire cassettes with cartoons which I couldn't wait to watch.

THE RATIONS

The Telecolor was considered a luxury good for the simple reason that the food was the real issue. We started having less and less food starting with the second half of the eighties. You could notice the increased scarcity from the shelves of our Alimentara food shop where once you could find some sorts of salami, *parizer* and sausages. Now the shelves were completely empty, decorated with labels and tags in the memory of the old times. The Rations Era has begun.

Based on his personal doctor advice Iulian Mincu, Ceau□escu imposed the 'rationalized alimentation system' or better 'the scientific alimentation' for which a healthy person shouldn't consume more than 2.800 calories per day. They also gave other figures about the yearly consumption per person, like: not more than 60–70 kilos of meat, 8–10 kilos of fish, 260–280 eggs, 210–230 kilos of milk and dairy products except butter, 85–95 kilos of fruits, 70–90 kilos of potatoes.. You make the maths! He also affirmed in a conference of The Executive Committee of the Socialist Party in July 1982, before the publication of the document, that he didn't take away food from the population but he was giving. He also said that was anyone's choice to eat more than that, but on his own risk could die earlier. His wife completed by saying: 'Well, we are publishing the documents with the correct guidance, if they want to follow it is their choice, if they don't is their risk!'

In the next period, the Government directives were already active: the citizens were instructed, the shelves went empty and the queues became longer. In two years' time after this document, Ceausescu and his 'scientific team,' worked up a new health population program: the necessary consumption of meat was reduced at 39 kilos per year, the eggs one at 120, the dairy products at 78 kilos and the fruit and veg one at 66 kilos.

In 1985 the shop assistants in our food shop, had to sell the food following the lists with names contained in a massive register. Pages and pages of charts, divided per months and food sort. Each family belonging to our area, had a designated page each month, like this was easier for them to distribute the monthly rations. The quantities were allocated based on the numbers of family members. Those sporadic queues in front of the food shop were swapped by the new system and there was no more reason for them to exist. Only one infinite queue in my vision, by the end of each month in order to get the food allocated by the Government for each family. As they decided to give us less food, was easier for them to manage the stocks in order to save more money and resources. Starving the population was the right political choice beside the cold and the scarcity of other primary resources.

With an ID in hands and few recycled plastic bags, like the beautiful white ones with the logo 'I love NY' proudly produced for exportation in our local plastic factory, in exchange of a signature and some money, Romanians could come back home with a poor stock which had to last for a month at least. Each person had the right in my area at least for 1 litre of rancid oil made of all sort of seeds (you should supply the bottle in order to get it), one hundred grams of salami, 500 grams of cheese, 10 eggs, 500 grams of row meat (pork or cow), 1 kilo of chicken legs, wings, heads, half kilo of flower and half kilo of corn flower, hundred grams of butter, one kilo of sugar and half kilo of rice all of them based on availability. Most of the times the stock was insufficient, especially for meat, cheese and oil. You couldn't complain about it and was more a question of luck. In some occasions, the shop managers, in order to please everybody, decided to halve the rations of those products in lack, despite the anger of some protesters.

To get the meat, you had to queue as before in front of the butcher shop for days. The only difference was that now we had an allocated amount per person and wasn't anymore on the shop assistant discretion the maximum amount per person. Romanians used to call the pig legs 'Adidas' and their heads 'calculators' as these parts were a popular supply. Same for the turkey's bones called hilariously 'Japanese *tacamuri*' and chicken legs. They were considered meat as well. Our mothers were super chefs and they managed to cook from nothing the most delicious soups and meals. The soup, in our culinary tradition is the first course which was an advantage as a soup could last for one week in the fridge in between the ups and downs of the electricity supply. Usually was over boiled hence its good conservation. As I already anticipated in a previous chapter, we were lucky because of my father's calories monthly supplements. We passed with dignity all that dark period of our lives. More than this, we had few good connections at the slaughter house, in a farm in the country side and never been in lack of food. There was a quote at the time saying that 'had more value a connection in communism than e property in Capitalism.'

We had potatoes every evening, were the exact image of 'Potato Eaters' of Caravaggio. That painting awakes always sad feeling and emotions in my brain. They were a great side dish in my family but for some people they were the only main dish they could have. Boiled, fried, baked, mashed, squished they became the foundation in our culinary habits.

Home baked cakes wasn't contemplated in the 'scientific health program' so was difficult sometimes to find the right ingredients in order to make a decent cake. Once, my mom, following Bogdan and Sandu kind requests to make a caramel cake, decided to do it despite of lack of some basic ingredients, as butter. As a result the caramel in between the layers became hard as concrete and the only way to cut the cake was by using the hummer. Initially she wanted to throw it away, but she couldn't because the two droll insisted to have a slice at any cost. Once she managed to cut a couple of pieces, she throw it away. The 2 little brothers, managed to take away the big block of cake from the garbage and they hide it in their school bags. They took it to kindergarten the following day to show off in front of their mates. The teacher, seeing the massive piece of cake, asked them to divide it with the other kids. Despite their unsuccessful attempt to cut it at the end Bogdan decided to tell her the trick: 'well, you can't cut it with the knife, our neighbour uses the hummer!' Of course, the story came on my mother ears and she felt so embarrassed. Then she decide to not improvise anymore and to make cakes only when she had all the ingredients. Wise choice!

Someone says that if the Romanians managed to overcome that nasty period, it was thanks to the connections system, the brave workers from factories of all sorts who dared to hide and bring home some products from the production line in order to re–sell them or to feed their families. I know that my mom's friend Florica, who was working on a day by day basis contract at Avicola (the chicken farm), was bringing us eggs and sometimes a chicken or a hen, Mariana was a shop assistant in the milk and dairy shop and under the counter she was selling us some milk, cottage cheese and butter and many like them were our precious connections.

The friends and acquaintances had a very important role in our lives during those times, because they were in direct contact with the food supplies. Our neighbour from the second floor, Mrs. Dragos, when she received any yummy gift from her patients, she was happy to share it with us. We were often invited for dinner in her house and that was the maximum of entertainment for us: sharing the food around a table of trusted friends.

Chapter 5

LIFE CHANGING REMOVALS

IN THE PROVINCE

Following the restoration of an old military base, in 1985 my father had a higher job offer as the Commander of the Aeronautical Military Base in a small town about 1 hour and half distance from Buzău, in the Eastern part of the country on the border with Soviet Union. By accepting this position, we had to commit to all the rest: changing house, neighbours, connections and me, school and friends.

This wasn't a great news for me as a teen. Renouncing on all my friends was sad and heart breaking. I was on year eight at the time, which in Romanian education system is the last year of Secondary School. I was aspiring to leave in Bucharest at the time, not in a smaller city than mine with less opportunities in my opinion, no Universities, theatres and shopping centres.. But I had no choice and my opinion wouldn't have affected my parents decision. Like this, I found myself in the last two terms of my year eight, in a new classroom, with new mates, new teachers, completely different accent, which was funny somehow for me and a much smaller city. That academic year was important also because at the end of it I had to take the exam of admission in the High School. There were only three good High school to go for and the most prestigious was the next door school of Mathematics and Physics profile. Was renowned for the outstanding results and high standard education and very strict teachers. Most of my new class companions would've gone for it so did I.

My father became a sort of public figure in the city and part of the local Politicians lobby. Not something to be proud of, but he was part of the system and couldn't deny it. The problem was that my father wasn't a party guy, he was very strict and incorruptible not quite a positive quality for the corrupted politicians of the time.. Unfortunately, pushed by the system he became a sort of political connection and wasn't very comfortable with that position at all. His assistant Commander, Major Vulpe (Fox), was thinking to be the perfect guy for that position and for this reason the relation between the two was conflictual and not so nice. As if that weren't enough, he was living in the same building with us and between me and his two children of my age, was running the same bad blood.

By restoring that old military base which ceased to function no longer after the WWII, the Government activated to build new houses for the military personnel due to their arrival in short time. They demolished, an old area of houses in the proximity of the city centre and they built these beautiful villas with two floors, red roofs and eight apartments each. This area was standing up from the city skyline and design, by its new and modern architecture. Living in one of these apartments within the 'Villa's Neighbourhood' was reason to be categorized as a posh or politically important person. Despite the fact this area was designated only for military, due to some civil connections, not all the apartments have been allocated to my father's colleagues. Some directors, doctors and politicians got them too but also some old people whose houses were on that land before the demolition. My father had the opportunity to choose the best option for our family since the project was only on paper, so we end up in this beautifully designed apartment on the second floor like this we wouldn't have anybody else living above us to disturb.

My bedroom was facing the courtyard of my Secondary School and I was quite excited about it. I could see not only the school yard but also the opposite villa. On that side of the building my neighbours had the kitchens and I could see almost everything was happening in those people houses, which was fun. The first floor neighbours, an old couple, used to stay around the kitchen table after midnight, listening to Free Europe or The Voice of America radio stations. I think they were deaf because I could clearly hear from my bedroom all the intermittent croaky programmes they were listening to. I was studying till late and they made me so much company during my High School years.

My father finally had his dream basement, dry, supplied with electricity, no mosquitos, big enough for wood, tools and food storage, proper stairs not wobbling ladders and of course the biggest available one within the building. We didn't have central heating but we had beautiful traditional terracotta fireplaces as a wonderful feature for each room. That was an innovation from the architecture point of view, also because the wood was much less expensive than the gas and also widely available especially with all the new connections in place we had at the time.

ANOTHER NEW SCHOOL

My new school, where I supposed to study for the last two terms of the year eight, was conveniently located just on the back of our villa. Somebody was thinking to create a hole in the fence of the back yard, like this my trip to school was only few minutes long and not fifteen as it would've take to follow the proper route.

Due to my good results, I was placed in the best classroom of year eight, a sort of nerds' classroom. Our desks were accommodating two pupils and there was no desk available for me a part one where was sitting a boy. Oh dear, a boy! His name was Victor, smart, especially in Maths, perky and very cute as well. Sometimes he used to drag me in his messes during the lessons and the teachers used to punish me as well. He was also very spiteful and during the lessons his hands finished touching my legs and that was making me jumping from my place in the middle of the lessons. He liked to still my notebooks and to write love messages on their last page. Sometimes he just mess around leaving stupid drawings on the empty pages. I used to tell him off to my teachers and sometimes he ended by being interrogated in front of the blackboard. I wasn't always happy to tell him off, also because I liked him a little. He brought a tulip once too! The French teacher understood the sort of connection there was between us and he used to make jokes on us in front of the whole classroom, pretending that we were a proper couple. Victor was very good in French, which for me was a real problem, as in my previous school in Buzău I studied only English starting with year five and German language starting with year six. In this school they've started with French in year five and English from year six, so they were quite advanced for me. In other classes Russian was another option but no German. My father asked the Head Teacher of the school to have extra lessons of French in order to get decent votes and he agreed. My French teacher was giving me supplementary French lessons twice a week in a studio put on our disposal by the head teacher for free. The lessons weren't free so I had to pay him cash each time I was having a lesson.

Victor was my first friend in the new classroom but soon I made friendship with Adina. She was the first for results in our classroom, daughter of a land troupes military and she was my best friend almost for the whole duration of the high school till her father was transferred for e better job position in Bucharest and me in a different city.

We had many things in common Adina and me: both were military daughters, with big passion for singing and poetry, little nerds and above all we both with the aspiration to get into Academy of Economics Study in Bucharest at the University. The admission exam was very tough and we were talking about a competition of 20 candidates fighting for one place as the number each year was limited. We knew that we had to work hard and we organised a study plan to work through.

Since she became my friend, I preferred to walk back home

after school, following the long path as she was living half way. Wasn't a long walk together but enough to talk about very important things. We were whispering about politics. Aware of the fact that something was wrong in our political system, trusting enough one in each other, we weren't afraid to talk about all the observations we could make at the age of 14, 15 and 16 years old. We knew that something had to change and we were confident that 'something soon had to happen.' Was in the air!

MAYBE FIRST LOVES

While in my previous classroom in Buzău I had many admirers equals many tulips, in this classroom I had much less. Firstly, because we didn't know each other, secondly because there were few beautiful competitors too and thirdly because now I was 14 years old and my father wouldn't allow me to talk about a boy.

A part from Victor, who teased me with his jokes, there was Leonard, a shy blonde boy, with blue big eyes and freckles on the white teenager cheeks. Wasn't as cute as Victor but he had a crush on me and he was writing me beautiful poems. He was a very talented writer and I saved all the poetry and short stories he wrote me in those last moths of year eight. All his writings were dedicated to me and he even wrote me the lyrics for the song I had to sing for the National Competition 'The Singing of Romania' where my school won a place. I liked him, despite the fact we never had the courage to talk about our feelings. Never a kiss, only glances and poems, beautiful poems. He will always have a place locked there in my heart.

I had a secret admirer too who I suspected was from a different class. He used to leave me paper messages with love declaration and a terrible grammar and calligraphy. I never knew who he really was but was my only secret admirer and was also funny.

HIGH SCHOOL ADMISSION

The end of the secondary school was meaning the beginning of the way to maturity. This is how they used to call the high school a vault for the future, for who you really wanted to become in life. Taking it seriously was a choice you had to think from the start and you had to have clear ideas about after: University path in my case. I was grown up with my mom's theory to 'become somebody in life' and that, on her opinion and many others, was the only way.

The high school in Romania, wasn't a must for everybody. Only the first 8 years were at that time compulsory, first exam to get in and after 2 years you had the option to go ahead for the last two years by passing an exam or to stop there and to follow a low skill qualification career. The exam to get into the High School was called First Step and was made of two exams all over the country: Mathematics (Algebra and Geometry) and Romanian (Grammar and Literature). After two years was followed by the Second Step exam and by the baccalaureate at the end of the whole 4 years, probably the equivalent of GCSE's. Life started to be tougher because of the exams and studying became a sort of mission for me with long nights on books and less time for friends.

The next door High School with a Naval Industry Profile, was my target and Adina's too. Was the most prestigious and renowned in town and passing the First Step with a high vote was very important to get in the best classroom, eventually the first one which was pure Mathematics and Physics profile. Despite all my efforts my 8.89/10 vote placed me only the ninth bellow the line and I got in the second classroom which was equally a good one considering there were eight classrooms in total. Adina was the first bellow the line and so luckily we end up as classmates again.

The competition was on and it would've be there to last for many years onwards. Victor got a place in the first class and that make me feel a bit sad but he was still in the same school with me and his classroom was only two doors away on the corridor of the first floor. In exchange I had many of my year eight colleagues in my classroom. Almost half of my old classroom was there and that gave me a sort of confidence. At the end our classroom was the coolest of the year, maybe because we were not only nerds, we were nerds but with a twist: a bit undisciplined, bold, daring and miles more funny. Being the first class of Navy Mechanics was less pressure than being the class of Maths and Physics but there was always competition between us. Our teachers had very high expectations on us also because that first classroom of Mechanics had the reputation to launch about

95% of its students in the University.

I've learned only after many years that all my classroom's mates end up with jobs as solicitors, engineers, doctors, managers, mathematics and physics teachers, university professors and even a judge. They all became 'somebody in life,' based on our standards and I was proud to be part of that bunch of people, even if that was for only 2 years.

THE UNIFORM

Once in the High School we finally left behind the Pioneer's uniforms. Now we had to wear for the special occasions, blue uniforms like soldiers. We were part of The Union of the Young Communists (called UTC) Trousers. Our day to day uniform was similar with the old one with the difference that instead of the red pioneer scarf around our neck, we had to wear a proper dark blue tie which made us feel more like grown–ups.

Long hair had to be tied up in a ponytail or a plat and we had to wear a white head band. The boys were allowed only with maximum one centimetre and a half long hair. The skirt couldn't be above our knees and boy's trousers couldn't be modified to be more in line with the fashion trend of the eighties. Only beige tights for girls and dark socks for boys. We all had an enrolment number with the name of the school which we had to wear on our uniform and on our coat as well.

Having all the uniform requested was meaning an important expense at the beginning of the year for each family. Daily uniform, the UTC uniform, the sport activities outfit, the lab uniform, winter coat, autumn coat in dark colours and adequate shoes for each. On top of these we had to pay for all the books, stationery, notebooks and schoolbags. To not be forgotten the classroom found to be paid at the beginning of the year too. The school used to supply free books which had to be returned by the end of the year, but their conditions were really bad, reason I always had to buy them brand new.

For the beginning of the academic year 1987–1988, my mother bought me a beautiful red coat for winter time. Was a long waterproof warm coat. Just perfect for our freezing winters with temperatures 16 degrees below zero sometimes. I just couldn't wait to wear it for school. My mother sewed the enrolment number on my left sleeve, as that coat was designed to be worn the whole winter on my ways to school. The day I put it on, once arrived at the school gate I couldn't pass the uniform control and I've been sent home in tears. The reason was its colour: red wasn't appropriate for school, we had to wear 'earth colours' as they called beige, brown, blue, grey and black. I had to stay at home that day because that was my only winter coat. I had to wait for my father return from work to go to the shop and buy a new 'appropriate' coat.

That day was my birthday too.

SWEET SIXTEEN

The daily life inconvenience became a routine for all of us. But when you are sixteen, despite the fact that most of my time was dedicated to my studies, I felt inside the irrepressible need to listen to music. Trivial as it may seem, for me and Adina, music was a vital necessity. We both loved to sing and to listen to music, the real music, the one sang in English language.

In March 1972 was founded the The Third Program of the Romanian Broadcasting dedicate to the youth. Was the first interactive radio station in Romania, an avant–garde station during the communist period, the place where the 'generation in blue jeans' was born and evolved. The third Program was a breath of fresh air during the last communist regime, a bold post with special atmosphere that gathered around it young people like me and Adina, people who loved theatre and music.

That program was revolutionary also because was the only place where politics wasn't contemplated and the only radio with live broadcasting which was an absolute novelty. There were shows like Musical Varieties, The Hit of The Day, The Teenagers Club, The Curious Club, The Ideas Chronical, The Folk Geography, The Disco House, Radio Super–Top, poetry and live broadcasts from the country. From 6 pm for about one hour, I remember was my favourite broadcast: Music Panoramic. They used to play music from abroad and the most popular songs in other countries like United Kingdom, Unites Stated, France or Germany. Then was Pittis Show, late in the evening on the theme of rock music, history and evolution of musical styles. The show was named by his author, Florian Pittis who was a stage and television actor, theatre director, folk music singer and radio producer. He had a very active life and he was loved both by his own generation and by the youth. He was called many superlative and admirative names as 'the prophet of the blue–jeans generation' and 'the most beautiful voice of the Romanian theatre'.

After lessons, on our way back home, I and Adina were talking about the new songs and how we could catch up the words to may sing them too. There wasn't much entertainment for us at that age. The only way we could get together was going to a birthday party. They were organised at home on Saturday or Sunday. Usually they started at 4 or 5 pm to be finished not later than midnight based on age of course. The living room was the perfect scenario for these events which for the occasion was decorated and all the furniture moved to make space for the dancing area surrounded by chairs. Some boys were happy to bring their own music and to play it pretending to be the party DJ. No alcohol, no cigarettes admitted.

There was another way for me to have fun, and this was by participating to after school Literature Club. The Club was 4 times a week on the back stage of our local Theatre. Tovarasha Tomescu, our lovely teacher of Romanian Literature, proposed me and encouraged me to participate. Her lessons were a pleasure for the ears and soul. She was a tiny lady, with white hair caught in a bun on the back of her head, with blue eyes and velvety skin. She was near to her retirement but also recognized as one of the best teachers of

Literature in town. Her lessons were like meditation for us, we forgot about the outside world, and her passion made us love even more our big poets and writers. Once she said that our year 10 Literature manual was so good that if we could rip off the first two pages with the images of Ceau□escu, the book could have an honourable place in any decent library.

She appreciated me a lot as a student and had a weakness for me, so she tried to encourage me to follow the Drama studies (IATC – The Institute of Theatrical and Cinematographic Arts) at the University as she was thinking I could succeed in a theatre career. That was a great idea but the admission was double difficult than the one for the Economics Studies. The oral exam for Drama faculty was terrifying and people used to tell the stories of the weird interrogations and unexpected questions students had to answer without blinking twice. It was in my head for a while but at the end I decided to go for my initial path and follow my brain instead of my heart.

She knew how to bring magic in our lessons and once she borrowed the school recorder to may play the Seasons of Vivaldi vinyl. Was heavily snowing outside and she said that was the perfect time to listen The Winter of Vivaldi with the promise to listen The Spring during the spring and so on. If somebody will ask me to think of a happy moment from my past to think about, I'll think of that Literature lesson during winter time accompanied by those magical notes. The complete silence created was amplifying the vinyl imperfections, and despite the freezing cold in our classroom, all of a sudden I had the feeling of being in front of a massive fireplace, in a muffled room, watching the dance of the snowflakes falling outside the window.

There was no rush, all things had to happen on their own time, and we had to learn to be patient and to wait the right seasons to may listen for the right music.

THE SINGING OF ROMANIA

Cantarea Romaniei or literally 'Song (of praise) to Romania' was an annual national cultural festival intended to promote ideologically– approved artistic manifestations, featuring both professional and amateur artists from across the country as defined by Wikipedia. In Ceau□escu's mind that was the right way to promote the National communism in Romania and shape the national identity of the Romanians starting with young generations like us.

Was a massive event dedicated to education and socialist culture with an educational, political, ideological impact, organised in phases just as a competition with a third, second and first classified. The lower level was between schools within the same town. Only the most important single act would've been promoted to pass to the next level between Regions ending up with the National level which was filmed and broadcasted on television.

When initially was proposed in 1976 after the Culture and Socialist Education Congress, its unique scope was to promote only the popular and rural art and not the cultural and modern one which wasn't considered a model to be followed in our president mentality.

Our Highs School was the owner of a long tradition toffees regardless this festival and they were all proudly displayed on the ground floor in front of the main entrance.

That was the perfect occasion to show off my talent as a singer and actress too, and for nothing in the world I would've missed it. I've been selected for a part in a traditional play filled with folk songs and poetry and as a singer too. When rehearsals time arrived, we had to commit with many daily after school hours. Was exhausting but also a lot of fun and all our efforts have been paid with the selection for the next Regional competition level. Our play and my song, both have been selected so we had to travel, spend a couple of nights somewhere and be ready to perform at the highest level. The song I had to perform was literally my song. I wrote the music and remember Leonard? The blonde boy with freckles who was writing me poetry when I was in year 8? Well he wrote the words for me and of course was a love song, a beautiful love song of which I remember only the first two lines unfortunately: 'When red butterflies will cry into your palms, Shining the borders of the lily..'

As we qualified for the final, the pressure became higher and the rehearsals longer and longer. We were tired but still happy and excited. For the play we had to wear traditional costumes and for my performance I had to wear white shirt and black skirt. As nowhere was written of which fabric the skirt had to be made, my mother designed for me a beautiful black tulle skirt with a satin belt tight in the middle with a crystal brooch. My hair wasn't long that time unfortunately because was happening at a short period of time after that fight with my mother when I locked myself in my bedroom and I cut my hair for the desperation. But for the rest I was looking good and I was allowed to wear heals as well. My singing didn't betray me and I arrived in the final.

We arrived in the final with our folklore play too, and we were qualified with a first place for the direction and interpretation. Great result for our school and for the entire city. I was qualified with a third place for my song and interpretation. The only reason I was dreaming for a first place was because only with e first place qualification on this event, you could participate to our annual singing national contest, 'The Unnamed Star.' That was the most important pop music contest and participating would've opened your gates to a successful singing career. Deep inside that was always my forbidden dream: to become a professional singer. I knew that wasn't a way to 'put bread on my table' as a grown up, but I always tried to pursue my dream in parallel with my academic studies.

THE SPORT

I always liked sports and in my little world I was a sportive too. My first sport I have practiced was gymnastics and this was thanks to Nadia Comaneci who in 1976 won at the Montreal Olympics three golden medals and the unforgettable zero point zero zero as the electronic display wasn't designed for figures higher than nine point nighty nine as she got a ten out of ten. In 1979, Nadia was awarded with the title of Hero of the Socialist Work in a broadcasted national event. She was an example for our generation and as a child I was dreaming travelling like her, winning medals and being awarded and famous in my country.

I was doing gymnastics for a couple of years when I was 7 or 8 years old but wasn't quite my talent. So I went for the artistic ice skating but I did it just for fun not for competitions. I took ballet classes too, but I was considered too old at 11 years for a ballerina career. Usually that was a career to be started at 5 years old and there was special border school in Bucharest for aspiring ballerinas where one of my mother cousins was formed since young age. I had my 15 minutes of fame as a ballerina when we had to dance French Can–Can for the end of the year performance.

During my High School, I discovered that I could do something more than just a sport. And something more than a sport is an extreme sport. In this little town, Tecuci, where I was living and where the Aeronautic Military Base was under my father command, there was the most important Skydiving Centre called Smaranda Braescu. This lady was a parachuting and aviation pioneer and multiple world record holder. She was nicknamed the 'Queen of the Heights' and in 1928 she became the first Romanian woman to ever obtain a parachuting licence and one of the first women in the world to do so. She was originally from a village not far from our city and a pride for our community. As a brave pilot daughter, I was happy to proof my limits and to show my father my abilities. Being recommended in this sport wouldn't do much difference. Was all up to you and your physical abilities once alone in between the sky and earth. No connections needed, allowed or permitted there. The summer time, when was the perfect time and weather for jumps, was preceded by a long period of workouts and believe me they were like Marines workouts. I felt like soldier Jane from the renowned Ridley Scott movie for few years due to this passion and I was healthy like a horse. In the summer of the 1988 I made my first jump from an AN2 slow and heavy aeroplane from 900 metres with an AV28 parachute. Was followed by others but none of them as the fourth one.

We had to jump out the aeroplane based on our weight due to scientific physics reasons. As I was the smallest, I was always the last in the queue. It was my fourth jump when after I left the aeroplane, my parachute didn't open properly. Instead of a 57.4 sqm round surface above my head, I had only doughnuts of silky fabric mixed with ropes. My parachute wasn't folded in a correct way and later on I acknowledged that was folded with no supervision of a professional. I had to solve the problem in a very limited period of time: in seconds. My initial descent speed was about 5 metres per second to multiply with the acceleration. I had to act quickly in order to save my life. During the workouts and theory lessons, we never practice how to open the spare parachute, the little one positioned on the abdomen and I was afraid to pull the handle. My fear was that this second parachute could interfere with the main one, I was hanged on and I could worsen the situation. So I decided to work out the main parachute. In order to do so I had to use the force I think I never ever used in my life and I managed to pull and slide all the 28 ropes which were tangled with the silk fabric. By doing this, I managed to restore the round surface and to slow down my descending but I also managed to switch the surface upside down and my four principal belts, two for each shoulder which were holding 7 ropes each, reversed without possibility of manoeuvring my parachute. As I couldn't choose my landing point I had to leave myself to chance. And they were four chances beneath myself: a very busy road, a moody river, the railway and a field of mature corn two metres height at least corn. By chance I've been left just few metres away from the road in the middle of the corn field. My parachute was all over the place and the 28 six metres long ropes tangled in the middle of the long dry and yellow plants. With an extraordinary force, while crying for my relief of being alive, I managed to clear all the place and as a survivor in a final of an apocalyptic movie, I grabbed all the pieces and started my return to the base. There were farmers on the field next to the corn one, picking watermelons wondering where I was coming from, I was looking like an alien for them. They were saying while I was passing: 'Where are you coming from, child?' 'Where from with all those weights?,' 'Oh my God, look at that!.' I was only smiling on them proud to be me and for being able to make it through.

My father was informed about the accident, and he started to run towards me. I was the last one who left the aeroplane but the first one to arrive on Earth, few kilometres away from our target landing point. He had tears in his eyes but happy to see me. He patted me on the back and we walked in silence till the military base. Despite the gravity, this episode passed unobserved, no sanctions, no responsibilities, no responsible, no insurance, no comments at all. Only curious eyes and people whispering and wondering about what was just happened. As 'nothing' has happened I continued to do my jumps that summer and the year after without other accidents.

ON THE THRESHOLD OF 1989

After the Step two exam at the end of the first two years of High School, my father received a new job offer in a bigger city, Focsani. He could refuse it but he didn't because on a hand, my mother wasn't quite happy in that little town and on another hand because his inactivity as a potential 'connection' wouldn't have helped the right people. In conclusion he wasn't considered useful for the political system. His working ambient became toxic for him, so he accepted the lower position in exchange of peace of mind and a much peaceful life. I was the only one in the family to feel sorry this time. For my colleagues, for Adina, for my extreme sport passion, for my Literature teacher and because Focsani wasn't Bucharest, the place I wanted to be.

The last two years of the High School, year 11 and year 12 were the most important years in terms of study. The new school was not bad but the level of the classroom I was transferred in, was far from the level I left behind. I had great Literature, Chemistry and Philosophy teachers. As about my Maths teacher, I can't say the same thing. I used to go to this

Maths teacher home, which was renowned as the best Maths teacher in town to take extra lessons to may understand the new concepts and Maths challenges. I had to work really hard in order to pass the future exams with good results. Mathematics was one of the Baccalaureate exam and nevertheless the main admission exam at the Faculty of Hotel Management. By the end of the high school I had a one metre height pile of notebooks, called Student Notebooks because they were huge: 100 A4 pages, with Algebra, Geometry, Trigonometry and Mathematic Analysis exercises.

Despite the unexpected low level of my classroom there was something good and his name was Alex. He was very handsome and also the most popular guy of our form. Dark hair, with a fringe on a side, dark eyes, tall, fit and very playful, he was always smiling and joking. I liked him a lot and he figured it out because he was always teasing me. He was a military son too, his father was working under my father's division, so we had something in common. I was pretty, hardworking and good in Maths. Soon my values have been recognized and allowed me to gain a place on my classroom's most popular group. One day he offered me a rose at school and stolen a kiss from me. The kiss, officialised somehow our relation of which I never was sure. Our relation was limited to a touch of hands and a kiss or two during a birthday party. I never been sure that he was my boyfriend or he had real feelings for me because he never revealed his love. For the desperation I remember I was going to our neighbour at the ground floor of my building of flats, a gipsy woman who was living there with all her numerous family to ask her to read me the future in tarots. Poor women, she was so nice and every time she was just enforcing the same predictions: he feels very connected to you and yes, he loves you. I was sleeping with his photograph under my pillow making a wish every evening before I went to bed to dream about him.

But he was also a distraction, considering the study pressure and the exams preparation. He was my first platonic love and I had the courage to ask him only after more than twenty years when we spoke once by phone if he ever loved me. Guess what? He said that I was his first love too and yes, he had the same feelings for me as I did for him. Only after all these years I've learned the lesson about how to open my heart and how important is to express your feelings and not suffer in silence. Love wasn't my priority and my mother became more and more frustrating for me. She was pushing me every minute to study only. My success in life became her ambition and she wanted to get a sort of payoff as she never graduated or had her own job. Alex was there like a constant in my life and his small attentions helped me to get through those two difficult years.

Suddenly, everything was happening around me became less important. The water, gas, electricity supplies, the candles, the rationed food, the connections, the collections, the uniform, the television, the new apartments, the neighbours and even the music, all became secondary. I often missed my mates from the other High School, my best friend Adina, our girlie talks about our hopes, future, love, visions, wishes. Sometimes I could hear music in the air, new notes, not exactly like Vivaldi's Winter Symphony. I remembered to watch first the sky when I got out from the house in the morning, as Mrs. Tomescu used to advise us. I remembered to hope that something one day could change for better as it did: was the Revolution's turn to change things, was 22nd of December 1989 and everything from a day to another would have been played on different notes. On those freedom notes everything changed but me.

About the author

Camelia Andrei was born on 25th of October 1972 in Buzau, Romania. She moved to Italy in 1995, where she completed two degrees in Tourism and Economics, at the University of Bologna. She moved to the United Kingdom with her two daughters in 2013, where she now pursues her passions as the owner of a themed tiny hotel and as a hypnotherapist. She continues to skydive once a year, and is still hoping to receive the tulip of her life..